New Grids on the Block

Hella '90s Crosswords

Edited by Francis Heaney

PUZZLE
WRIGHT
PRESS

New York

Contents

PUZZLE
WRIGHT
PRESS
New York

PUZZLEWRIGHT PRESS and the distinctive Puzzlewright Press logo
are registered trademarks of Sterling Publishing Co., Inc.

© 2023 Sterling Publishing Co., Inc.

ISBN 978-1-4549-5045-5

For information about custom editions, special sales, and premium purchases,
please contact specialsales@unionsquareandco.com.

Manufactured in Canada

2   4   6   8   10   9   7   5   3   1

unionsquareandco.com

Cover design by Melissa Farris
Cover and interior illustrations (pp. 3, 116, 125) by Fionna Fernandes
Cover background by Lyubov Vigurskaya/Shutterstock.com

Introduction

Different generations lived through many different versions of the '90s. I'm a Gen Xer, which means that not only is it very stereotypical of me to have waited until the last minute to be writing this introduction, but also that for me, the '90s were the years in which I was starting to figure out how to be an independent person—and writing my first crosswords. Meanwhile, I was watching all of "Seinfeld," fully indulging in the swing dancing revival, and listening to many indie bands on the Sub Pop label whose oeuvres regretfully do not hold up very well. (There were some keepers, though! Velocity Girl's "¡Simpatico!" is one for the ages.)

But then there are Millennials, who understand a lot of things that only '90s kids will understand, which is why I sought out some of them to contribute to this book. There are post-Millennials represented here as well. After all, younger generations remember the '90s, too—much in the same way that I remember the '50s and '60s: from soaking up our parents' tastes, or from retro TV shows (a long and proud tradition from "Happy Days" to "That '70s Show" to, uh, "That '90s Show").

All that's to say that whether you were watching Nickelodeon or "NewsRadio" in the '90s, there's something here for you! And since my goal was to capture different perspectives, I've tried to preserve each puzzlemaker's individual voice, which means you'll find a lot of variety throughout the book, both in terms of style and subject matter. Generally speaking, the puzzles start out on the easy side and will get trickier as you proceed, finishing up with a challenging themeless crossword packed with '90s pop culture.

Happy puzzling! I gotta bounce.

—Francis Heaney

Fashion Statement

BY ZHOUQIN BURNIKEL

ACROSS

1 "To ___ it mildly ..."
4 "Titanic" or "Jurassic Park," for example
8 Winter road application
12 They might clash in a boardroom
14 Prefix similar to "ultra-"
15 Toddler's boo-boo
16 Collar adornment popular in the 1990s
19 Women's ___ movement
20 Imposes, as a tax
21 Wrist ornament popular in the 1990s
26 Enjoy some Lunchables, say
27 Aang's flying bison in "Avatar: The Last Airbender"
28 "What ___ we going to do?"
29 Hair bands popular in the 1990s
35 One under an advisor's wing
37 Like Mandarin Chinese
38 Love to pieces
39 All keyed up
40 Wrist ornaments popular in the 1990s
44 Repeated cheer in Chumbawamba's World Cup 1998 song "Top of the World"
45 "Dirty Jobs" host Mike
46 Pickleball court divider
47 Bill holders popular in the 1990s
52 Lizard with a dewlap
54 ___ Angeles Sparks (team founded in 1997)

55 Hair fasteners popular in the 1990s
61 Lake south of Lake Huron
62 Letter opener?
63 "Twin Peaks" star ___ Flynn Boyle
64 Large wine casks
65 Puts in stitches
66 Silent acknowledgment

DOWN

1 Chest muscle, briefly
2 "How disgusting!"
3 "You snooze, you lose!"
4 Chinchilla coat
5 "Son of," in Arabic names
6 "Malcolm X" director Spike
7 Magic Eraser pitchman
8 Complete, as a crossword puzzle
9 Sit tight for
10 Real head-scratchers?
11 Pegs at a driving range
13 Vinyl record problem
17 Recede, as tidal waters
18 "Kenan & ___" (sitcom that debuted in 1996)
21 Nautical chart
22 Texas border city with a Jalapeño Festival
23 Turkey trot, for one
24 First 30-day mo.
25 PC component
29 One gazing into a crystal ball
30 Stack on a pallet: Abbr.
31 Garden bed digger
32 Jakarta native

33 Baby bird of prey
34 Precipitates cold pellets
36 Uno e due
39 Ancient Greek theaters
41 Herding dogs originally from France
42 Time span a human can never personally experience
43 "Such a cute kitty!"
47 Interrupt at a dance
48 Finds utterly intolerable

49 Hydrocarbon suffix
50 Inc. alternative
51 Relax in a hammock
52 "Yeah, sure!"
53 Sikh spiritual leader
56 Membership charge
57 Ally McBeal's profession
58 Twelve-mo. spans
59 Turned ___ (emulated Tiger Woods in 1996, say)
60 Feeling down in the dumps

Answer on page 104.

Seasoned Performers

BY OLIVIA MITRA FRAMKE

ACROSS

1 Queer icon played by Lucy Lawless
5 Spins a hoop on one's hips, say
10 "G.I. Joe" segments that ended with "And knowing is half the battle!"
14 Qui-Gon Jinn and Obi-Wan Kenobi, for two
15 Genre of Adult Swim's "Toonami" block
16 "Rocket Power" character with a palindromic name
17 "Scream" spoof
19 President's annual delivery to Congress: Abbr.
20 Ms. Frizzle's vehicle of choice
21 Lug (around)
23 Default font on early Windows computers
26 Jan. 1 or Jun. 19, e.g.
29 "Good ___" (Terry Pratchett and Neil Gaiman novel)
30 Alternative to Sprite, in a Shirley Temple
32 Something Anakin Skywalker hates, in a memorably cringy scene
33 Caribou cousin
34 Book keeper?
36 Tofu base
39 Gold digger's tool
43 Go along with
45 Tommy or Dil, to Stu and Didi
46 L.A., but not San Diego
48 Porsche Cayenne Turbo, for one
51 One way to serve pastrami
52 Lust, but not love

53 ___ Entity (Tina Turner's "Mad Max: Beyond Thunderdome" role)
54 Opposite of "received by," in a financial transaction
56 "Star Trek" series with Capt. Picard
57 Canada-based shoe brand
58 Group of five singers whose nicknames were coined by Top of the Pops magazine (and can be found in this puzzle)
65 Throw, as dice
66 "___ en Rose" (Edith Piaf song)
67 Buckeye State
68 Anti-dandruff shampoo
69 Setting for "The Little Mermaid"
70 Brewer's need

DOWN

1 Classic Jaguar convertible
2 Common Market inits.
3 "Don't spill the beans" document: Abbr.
4 Crash pad?
5 Thespians that overdo it
6 Colorful card game
7 She played Grace in "Armageddon"
8 "Who ___ to judge?"
9 Witnesses
10 Online marketplace for clothing
11 Like Rembrandt's "The Storm on the Sea of Galilee," in 1990
12 Show up
13 Minestrone, gazpacho, etc.
18 Christmastide
22 Sine's reciprocal, in trig
23 Eras

24 ___ Kiley ("Portions for Foxes" band)

25 Like a starless sky

26 Rock climber's need

27 Barcelonian "Bravo!"

28 Seized, as an opportunity

31 Bring up the ___ (trail behind)

35 Christian known for black clothing

37 Dress style named after a type of lingerie

38 Crane cousin

40 NAACP part: Abbr.

41 Cross off

42 Reason to go green?

44 Prefix with center

46 Like early synthesizers

47 It will hold your horses

49 Drink that's out of this world?

50 "Blue-Eyes White Dragon" trading card game

51 Mind-bending poster genre

55 European city that includes the Grünerløkka district

56 Nirvana's "Smells Like ___ Spirit"

59 MoveOn.org, e.g.

60 Linkin Park's "What ___ Done"

61 Org. memorably broken into in "Mission: Impossible"

62 Greek letter aptly found in "chapter house"

63 It may get glossed over

64 Song with the lyric "When you're gone, how can I even try to go on?"

Answer on page 104.

Step by Step

BY TONY ORBACH

ACROSS

1 ___ around (snoop)
5 Licorice-flavored seed
10 Start of Lauryn Hill's education?
13 Bind up with kitchen twine
15 Desert home of Ben-Gurion University
16 Put on a show
17 Step introduced in a 1990 Digital Underground video
19 End for brain or brawn
20 Table protector
21 Loony
23 Stars, in "Le Petit Prince"
25 Reach, as a level of achievement
26 Vehicles for a barista's foam art
27 Step popularized by a 1990 Madonna video
29 Genre for Reel Big Fish
30 Approach
31 Step popularized by a 1990 Marcia Griffiths video
37 Team spirit
38 Monopoly foursome: Abbr.
40 Step introduced in a 1996 Los Del Rio video
43 Gorgon with very unruly hair
46 Show up
47 Powerful members of Tony Soprano's crew
48 Major in music?

49 Butt and pivot hardware
50 Cleveland cager, for short
51 Step introduced in a 1994 69 Boyz video
56 Poetic tribute
57 Streetcars
58 Put off
59 1991 Pearl Jam album named for Mookie Blaylock's uniform number
60 Premature
61 Drink brand with two lizards in its logo

DOWN

1 ___ degree
2 Tulsa sch.
3 Bottom line
4 Vivacious cleverness
5 Peruvian peaks
6 Tidy
7 Engine starter: Abbr.
8 "Gimme a ___"
9 Occurring someday
10 Tiki bar quaff
11 Traps during winter
12 Word before arm or suit
14 Subway gate
18 ___ Saint Laurent
22 Wombs
23 Trains encircling the Loop
24 Share of the proceeds
25 A really long time
27 "Ta-da!"

28 Back in the day
30 "___ Torino" (Clint Eastwood film)
32 Net note
33 Biden's sports car model
34 Compilation in "Finding Your Roots"
35 Performance piece a player might end on a roll
36 Gaelic
39 ___ Bernardino
40 The LiMu Emu or Geico Gecko, for example
41 Place to play Skee-Ball

42 "Scream" director Wes
43 Simba grows one during "Hakuna Matata"
44 Barely beat
45 Some tractors
47 "Get Ur Freak On" rapper Elliott
49 Webpage makeup
52 British pop singer Rita who wed Taika Waititi
53 Crew tool
54 Dog bred with a border collie to produce a Borador
55 Caustic cleaning compound

Answer on page 105.

Nick Names

BY AIMEE LUCIDO

ACROSS

1 Kala and Terk of 1999's "Tarzan," e.g.
5 Planning detail
9 It's bumped out of respect
13 Marine flatfish
14 Wyatt of the Old West
15 Sparkling Italian wine
16 Comedian who played Coach Calhoun in "Grease"
18 Button on a scale
19 Four Holy Roman emperors
20 Overzealous, as a fan
21 Scoundrel
23 "Schitt's Creek" star known for his eyebrows
26 ___ all-time high
28 Did some barre, perhaps
29 Gymnast Suni of Team USA
30 Put together
31 Word commented on a Reddit post, often with a caret beside it
33 "Motion Sickness" indie rocker
40 Home of the Blue Devils
41 "An American ___: Fievel Goes West"
42 Hinge or Bumble, e.g.
45 Alec's "Beetlejuice" co-star
48 Mlle., across the Pyrenees
49 Politician who became both president and vice president without being elected
52 Get-up-and-go
53 Dish made with corn, mayo, chili powder, and cheese

54 McEvoy of makeup
56 Attend
57 Nickelodeon show with a football-headed protagonist, or where you can find the characters at the starts of 16-, 23-, 33-, and 49-Across
61 Clarifying phrase
62 Humans, in the "Predator" franchise
63 Taylor-Joy of "The Queen's Gambit"
64 Portal for Mario
65 Tennis match parts
66 Open, as a banana

DOWN

1 Pompous sort
2 Luau bowlful
3 Mythical city of gold in an early DreamWorks movie
4 Offshoot group
5 Escort to the door
6 Turn a certain corner in a board game
7 Historic time
8 EMT's specialty
9 Like the most serious mistakes
10 "Violeta" author Allende
11 Endeavor
12 Do a colorful 21-Down activity
17 Stopped fasting
20 Renovated
21 Setting for "Indian Summer" or "Addams Family Values"

22 One of the Four Corners states

24 ___'acte

25 Soda brand since 1924

27 "I'm gonna ___ you to go ahead and come in tomorrow": "Office Space"

32 York and Pepper, for short

34 Taps blower

35 Stretched (out)

36 Ali Wong and Steven Yeun show about a grudge

37 Listening device

38 Solemn ceremony

39 Be phenomenal

42 Generational disparity

43 First female House speaker

44 "Speaking as someone with experience here ..."

46 "Wait a moment"

47 Computer data structures

50 Make amends

51 NE or SW, e.g.

55 Simple fastener

57 Some PCs

58 Before, in Shakespeare

59 Caustic solution

60 Indian lentil stew

Answer on page 105.

First-Class Males

BY TRIP PAYNE

ACROSS

1 Flutes and oboes, for example
6 "Gee, you DON'T say"
9 Company with the slogan "Free Your Pores!"
14 Numskull
15 Abbr. on a cornerstone
16 Result of successful upselling
17 Thrower of throwing stars
18 1990
20 1997
22 Baz Luhrmann, for one: Abbr.
23 Paramount Network, originally
24 1942 battleground
28 Word before bar or blanket
30 Symbolic birds of "Twin Peaks"
34 "___ you just the cutest thing!"
35 Broadcast
37 Snicker from Beavis or Butt-head
38 Magazine award won by 18-, 20-, 51-, and 58-Across in the indicated years
41 "I'm ___ real jam here"
42 What an express minimizes
43 Utterly beat
44 Org. whose Endeavour first launched in 1992
46 High points
47 Ball girls?
48 Went ahead of
50 Strike zone determiner, for short
51 1991
58 1992
59 Get smart
61 "... sitting in ___, K-I-S-S-I-N-G"
62 Millennial's parent, perhaps
63 Three-card con game
64 Milk by-products
65 They, in Toulouse
66 Simple ghost costume

DOWN

1 Take the trophy
2 "Gotcha ... now let's keep enjoying this beat poetry reading"
3 Musical number?
4 Where a sensei teaches
5 Parts of Picard's logs
6 Stave off
7 Assn. that added a P for "Paralympic" in 2019
8 Webmaster's code
9 Lowest rung of British nobility
10 "Beats me"
11 Cartoon dog created by Jim Davis
12 Optimistic
13 Ending for propyl or acetyl
19 "Citizen Kane" actor Joseph
21 What a negroni has that a negroni sbagliato lacks
24 Washbowl

25 Where the action happens
26 State that was once a country
27 "Little Plastic Castle" singer DiFranco
28 Total pushovers
29 Long stretches
31 Move like a dervish
32 Overflow prevention
33 Lets one's hair down?
35 Straddling
36 Middle Eastern trees
39 Small apartment
40 Start of many rappers' names
45 Space bar neighbor, on a PC

47 Rolls-Royce's parent company
49 Sea eagles
50 Tech support callers
51 Heart of the matter
52 4,840 square yards
53 XXIII × VII
54 Company whose first compilation was "25 Country Hits"
55 "Everything Everywhere All at Once" star
56 "Titanic" actor Billy
57 Art Deco designer
58 "I reckon not"
60 Prefix for scape (as of 1994)

Answer on page 106.

"You Go, Girl!"

BY ZHOUQIN BURNIKEL

ACROSS

1 Matches in rings
6 Exam for an MBA hopeful
10 Shoe store chain
13 "Teenage Mutant Ninja Turtles" reporter O'Neil
14 Plane-tracking device
16 Earth-friendly prefix
17 Basketball player who was AP's Female Athlete of the Year in 1995
19 Mooch, as a ride
20 Unforeseen glitch
21 No longer troubled by
22 Curaçao neighbor
24 Figure skater who won the 1993 U.S. Figure Skating Championships
27 Pago Pago's place
28 "Exit full screen" key
29 Less contaminated
30 Cabo San Lucas's peninsula
33 Olympian Korbut
37 "How ___ things?"
38 Soccer player who was the U.S. Soccer Female Athlete of the Year from 1994 to 1998
41 "Yes, madame!"
42 Like an ostrich steak
44 Wander around
45 Same as always
47 Arroz ___ cubana
49 Bit of hijinks
50 Tennis player who won five Grand Slam singles titles in the late 1990s
56 Truism
57 Left on a ship
58 Spanakopita dough

61 "You betcha"
62 Speed skater who won four gold medals in the 1992 and 1994 Winter Olympics
65 Barley wine, e.g.
66 Looks for
67 "Jerry Maguire" co-star Zellweger
68 ID for a new U.S. citizen
69 Overly hasty
70 Roasted, as pollo

DOWN

1 Cell signal symbols
2 Australian ___ (tournament won by Monica Seles four times in the 1990s)
3 Metropolitan region
4 Extra innings are played to avoid one
5 Utah's capital, for short
6 Thanksgiving boatful
7 Rami with an Oscar for "Bohemian Rhapsody"
8 Think the world of
9 Browser opening
10 Fix, as faulty code
11 Underwater diving gear
12 "Have You Ever Really Loved a ___" (1995 Bryan Adams hit)
15 Howls with laughter
18 ___-Cola (company that installed a soda dispenser on the Space Shuttle in 1995)
23 San Juan, Puerto ___
25 Societal standard
26 Pack of printer paper
27 "Yeah, why not?"
29 Jerry Seinfeld, to George Costanza

30 Bun often filled and steamed
31 "I just got it!"
32 Spread for a scone
34 Its state flag features a pelican
35 Avocado dip, for short
36 Feel poorly
39 Persian Gulf nation
40 ___ bean (sprout source)
43 Western defense org.
46 Stops, as a yawn
48 Arms and legs
49 Initial poker stake
50 Chichen Itza residents
51 Jumps done by Michelle Kwan
52 Become ready to pick

53 Sleep clinic diagnosis
54 Protests on the road
55 Like the main characters of "The Commitments," "Michael Collins," and "In the Name of the Father"
59 Emulated the person who told The New York Times in 1992 that "harsh realm," "lamestain," and "swingin' on the flippity-flop" were popular grunge slang terms
60 Mini ___ (cookie introduced in 1991)
63 Opposite of 'neath
64 Garment with a racerback style

Answer on page 106.

Shuffle Play

BY REBECCA GOLDSTEIN

ACROSS

1 Flabbergasts
6 In a fitting way
11 Snappy reply
12 "Join us in the treehouse"
14 Symbol of proletarian solidarity
17 Falafel pockets
18 Dotcom field
19 Owl's yowls
21 Similar (to)
22 Singer-songwriter India.___
24 Nissan sedan
25 Shape on some playgrounds
29 Component of a stable diet?
30 Triage sites: Abbr.
31 Big yellow taxi, say
32 Liquid measured with a dipstick
33 Agrees silently
34 Portrayer of Elder Cunningham in "The Book of Mormon"
35 Guac and queso, e.g.
37 Red tag event
38 Bottom-heavy business model?
41 Eagle or emu, e.g.
42 Gross
43 Anticipatory night
44 Building block?
45 Cubes in some coffee
46 Application suffix
47 Kit ___ bar
50 100%
51 Character trope generally featuring frizzy hair, a lab coat, etc.
55 Noisy internet connection

58 Graduate degs.
59 Road trip game
60 Himalayan cryptids
61 In ___ of (rather than)
63 Photographer Adams
64 High-end stereo equipment of the '90s, and an alternate title for this puzzle
68 Brain cell
69 Pelvic floor exercises
70 Exhausted
71 Covered with powder, say

DOWN

1 Supply counterpart
2 They're pressed for money
3 Muppet introduced in 1993
4 Goof
5 Noise in the HBO opening sequence
6 "Thunderstruck" band
7 ___ Spice a.k.a. Victoria Beckham
8 "Pls stop telling me this"
9 Milk, in Mallorca
10 Smallest Canadian territory
11 Sine and cosine, for two
13 Inconsistency in a story, say
14 Trail blazer?
15 More than want
16 Fidelity alternative
17 Contact via beeper
20 Utters
22 Carne ___
23 Bone in a cage
24 Dijon seasoning
26 JibJab creation

27 "My bad!"
28 Catch-all category: Abbr.
33 First major hit for the Goo Goo Dolls
34 Greek wrap
35 Cut into cubes
36 "Beats me" on AIM
37 1995 thriller about the deadly sins
38 Is-thay anguage-lay
39 Flaky mineral
40 Curses
41 Contrary to popular ___
44 Animated cocker spaniel
45 Sprite
46 Ramadan festival
47 X's in an email

48 According to
49 "g2g!"
52 Blueprint detail
53 Converse All Stars, colloquially
54 Experiencing pins and needles
56 Mario gets more from mushrooms
57 Deplete
61 Den mother?
62 "And ___ it ironic? Don't you think?"
63 From the top
65 "Nuthin' But a 'G' Thang" rapper
66 Mother clucker
67 Fifth word of Weird Al's "The Saga Begins"

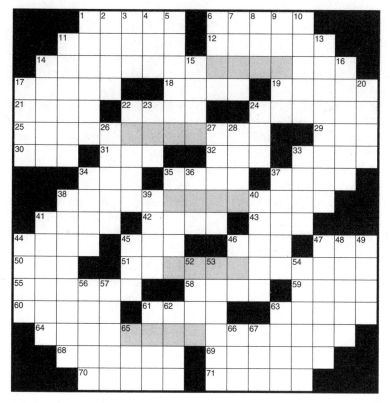

Answer on page 107.

Away Messages

by Nate Cardin

ACROSS

1 "I ___ your pardon!"
4 Pillow cover
8 Bio. or chem.
11 Mufasa's hair
12 Drug bust unit
13 "___ Croft: Tomb Raider"
15 "See ya," per "Terminator 2: Judgment Day" (1991)
19 ___ borealis
20 Unlike lucite heels
21 "___ your body down and wind it all around" ("Wannabe" lyric)
22 Just about
27 Minor criticisms
28 "See ya," per "Friday" (1995)
31 Keith Haring graffiti, e.g.
34 "The danger has passed"
35 Scatter seeds
38 "Scream" occurrences
40 Motor home campsite
42 Prenatal exam, briefly
43 Baby Spice Bunton
47 Shakespeare's feet
48 "See ya," per Green Day (1997)
51 Magilla Gorilla, for one
53 Colorful item in a pencil box
54 NFL six-pointers
57 Wine container
60 Distribute into groups
63 "See ya," per Sarah McLachlan (1995)
68 Thanks, in Berlin
69 Up to the task
70 Rose to one's feet
71 Farm or home add-on?
72 Migrant's vessel, often
73 Transports by truck

DOWN

1 Persian Gulf port
2 Put into a catacomb
3 Toothed wheel
4 The Mighty Mighty Bosstones' genre
5 Condition shared by Keith Haring, Ryan White, and "Magic" Johnson
6 "Aladdin" prince who's actually just Aladdin
7 "Black on Both Sides" rapper ___ Def
8 ___ on the back
9 Beachside place to change into a bathing suit
10 Resident of 1-Down
11 Attack savagely
14 Share a border with
15 Possesses
16 Guess Jeans, Versace, and Calvin Klein, for example
17 Hot Wheels product
18 "Absolutely!"
23 CIO partner
24 Red camcorder button: Abbr.
25 Plumbing pipe with a right angle
26 "I did not have sexual relations with that woman," for one

29 Search engine that debuted in 1994
30 Cowboy Hall of Famer Michael
31 Mathematician Lovelace
32 "Losing My Religion" band
33 Troll doll hair color, sometimes
35 "Likewise!"
36 Celestial sphere
37 There are 52 in a yr.
39 Mexican uncle
41 Campaign funding org.
43 Make a mistake
44 Actress Farrow of "Alice"
45 Physicians, for short

46 Suffix for drinks like Tang
49 Antlered animal
50 Saudi native
51 Chemicals used to "wash" jeans
52 Toy with, like a puppy might
55 Bib dribbles
56 Chippendales dancers, e.g.
58 ___-Seltzer
59 Ran from
61 Slangy word after jam or makeout
62 Miss, in Madrid: Abbr.
64 Listening organ
65 Wharton degree
66 One of Santa's helpers
67 "Have we ___?"

Answer on page 107.

Singing One's Praises

BY ELIZABETH C. GORSKI

ACROSS

1 First extra inning
6 Behave
10 Bartlett, for one
14 "Cavalleria Rusticana" baritone
15 "___ Want for Christmas Is You" (seasonal Mariah Carey hit from the "Merry Christmas" album)
16 Concerning
17 #1 Mariah Carey/Trey Lorenz single from the "Unplugged" album (1992)
19 Nero's 455
20 "The Sopranos" actress Falco
21 Belt-tightening hardware
23 Oodles
26 Victorian, for one
28 Bass brews
29 Famed cruise line
31 Literary categories
34 "Flashdance" singer Cara
35 Edmonton player
36 Aromatherapy spot
39 ___ Moines
40 #1 Mariah Carey single from the "Daydream" album (1995)
42 Chou En-___
43 Vane direction: Abbr.
44 Regular's bar order, with "the"
45 University of Maine locale
47 "Papa" Hemingway
49 Whine
50 Clarinet insert
51 Friendly leader?

53 Where heroes are made
54 Braces oneself
57 Oklahoma city
59 "High Voltage" rock band
60 Mariah Carey hit single from the "Merry Christmas" album (1994)
65 Polynesian feast
66 Actress Patricia
67 Neutral shades
68 Eyelid affliction
69 "Fifth Avenue" store
70 Backyard visitor you might nickname "Stinky"

DOWN

1 ___ chi
2 Right angle
3 Patriots' org.
4 Lhasa native
5 Did groundbreaking work?
6 "Politically Incorrect" host Bill
7 Land in la mer
8 Workers' rights org.
9 "Mon ___!" (French exclamation)
10 Sour slice on a sandwich
11 Mariah Carey/Luther Vandross hit single (1994)
12 Where Vincent van Gogh painted "The Night Café"
13 Guns the engine
18 Even
22 Plane passenger's tote
23 Etcher's needs

24 Entices
25 #1 Mariah Carey/Boyz II Men single from the "Daydream" album (1995)
27 Stir up
30 Tax returns?
32 Carrier to Tel Aviv
33 Nintendo game console letters
35 Burden of proof
37 "American Idol" jury
38 Garlicky mayo
41 Enzyme suffix
46 2013 sci-fi action film starring Vin Diesel

48 Save from disaster
49 Electronics giant
50 Edit further, as a film
52 Honeycomb compartments
54 Ladies
55 Eternities
56 Ellington's "Take ___ Train"
58 Juana ___ de la Cruz, poet of the Spanish Golden Age
61 Durable wood
62 Steve Carell's "Despicable Me" character
63 Attila, notably
64 "For shame!"

The Games of the '90s

BY ANNEMARIE BRETHAUER

ACROSS

1 Gratuity
4 Letter above W on the front of a '90s Eurovan
7 "Thanks, I ___ you one!"
10 King Kong, e.g.
13 Splicing it earned a 1993 Nobel Prize
14 Pub order
15 Bump on the tongue that may contain a taste bud
17 Mil. branch with ensigns and admirals
18 City that hosted the 1994 Winter Olympics
20 Plug away
22 Org. you might file an extension with
23 "Really ___!" (advice for sounding like a ghost, in "Beetlejuice")
24 City that hosted the 1992 Summer Olympics
27 "Cabaret" director
28 Disneyland's city
29 Sounded like a real boar?
31 "Dr. Quinn, Medicine Woman" production co.
32 He played Jim in 1991's "The Doors"
34 Government org. at Langley
35 City that hosted the 1992 Winter Olympics
40 Guadalajara gold
41 Adam Schiff et al., on "Law & Order"
42 Mid-11th-century date
45 Reducing activity
49 Scared stiff

52 What's stowed
53 City that hosted the 1996 Summer Olympics (and the first U.S. city to host after Los Angeles, CA)
55 Battle of Put-In Bay lake
56 Chi follower
57 Chinese leader Xiaoping
58 City and nation that hosted the 1998 Winter Olympics
62 Sue Grafton's "___ for Undertow"
64 Dubai or Qatar, e.g.
65 "Did ___ that?" (Urkel's catchphrase)
66 Direction from Stamford to New Haven, CT
67 IRS ID
68 LAX setting in winter months
69 "Batman" fight sound
70 Size above med.

DOWN

1 1989 play about Capote
2 Like some ramen
3 Museum landscape
4 Crooner Rudy
5 "Civil Wars" and "L.A. Law" character Levinson
6 Anago or unagi
7 Works such as 1991's "The Death of Klinghoffer"
8 Tot cries
9 Org. working to reduce pollution
10 "Missed by that much!"
11 Fill the bill
12 Justified
16 Utterly lacking in ethics
19 Architect Maya

21 I, in Innsbruck
24 "Batman" fight sound
25 Keep surviving
26 Actor Epps who played Linc in 1995's "The Mod Squad"
27 Shawarma wrap?
30 Chris O'Donnell police procedural show, for short
33 Business abbreviation in the U.K.
36 Choice for an uphill climb
37 Get-up-and-go
38 River in South Africa
39 French president Macron
43 Knee-to-ankle protector
44 Film director Lupino

45 "___ from a Mall" (1991 Bette Midler movie)
46 NFL team (when they weren't in Cleveland or St. Louis)
47 Kind of superhero story
48 Burner flame
50 "___ for something completely different"
51 Map abbr.
54 Carrere of "Wayne's World"
56 Some kiln pieces
59 One of many taken by a cat
60 "Great Expectations" hero
61 Lots of fuss
63 Match, as a poker bet

Answer on page 108.

Out at the Movies

BY TRIP PAYNE

ACROSS

1 1989 B-52's single that was the follow-up to "Love Shack"
5 "Cornflake Girl" singer Tori
9 Give a look-through
13 "Nessun dorma," for one
14 Product often described as "dolphin-safe"
15 Talk Like a Pirate Day greeting
16 1998 movie where Christian Bale played a gay music journalist
19 Phil DeVille's twin sister, on "Rugrats"
20 "___ Bayou" (1997 drama)
21 "RuPaul's Drag Race" champion Chachki
22 Word that can follow smart or dumb
23 Cartoon chihuahua of the 1990s
24 Gondolier's route
25 1996 comedy film set at a Florida drag club
28 Galoot
31 "Sister ___ 2: Back in the Habit"
32 It's picked out
33 Big brass
34 ___-182
37 Item in Trouble's Pop-O-Matic
38 Dowser's quest
39 Snort from a snout
40 Give the axe
41 Insta upload
42 "American Beauty" actor Bentley
43 1999 movie about a trans man in Nebraska
48 Social equals

50 "Concentration" pronoun
51 "The Crying Game" Oscar nominee
52 Mini-burger
54 Palookas
55 Darts player's asset
56 1990 documentary about New York City drag balls
59 Got down
60 Nutritionist's concern
61 Item with two racks, often
62 They're rolled up at the end of yoga class
63 Bohemian
64 Margaret Truman's mother

DOWN

1 Enthrall
2 Phrase promising vague consequences
3 Need quarantining, maybe
4 1994 Mel Gibson movie
5 Go to
6 Items in an office dishwasher, often
7 Co-founder of Artists Against Fracking
8 Recover from a wreck
9 Girl Scout cookie sold where the Caramel deLite isn't available
10 Relax
11 Top-tier
12 Putin's putdown
17 Rival of Navratilova
18 Wine and ___
19 Delt's neighbor

24

24 Meticulousness
26 Target of robberies in "Heat" and "Point Break"
27 Items found in many fountains
29 Mary Todd's husband, familiarly
30 Part of AFAIK
33 Good quality for an ambassador
34 Hawkeye's weapon
35 Trigger a polygraph
36 How a non-attendee might "be there"
37 Tiny fractions of a millennium
38 Person who might refer to nose and mouthfeel
40 Picador's contest

41 Lack during a blackout
43 Source of the "gold" in "Ulee's Gold"
44 Andy Brennan was one on "Twin Peaks"
45 Common origami constructions
46 Holds sway
47 Vegetable farmed in Nigeria
49 Reduces a sentence, maybe
52 Email involving Viagra, typically
53 In ___ land
54 Illegally assist
57 Honorary title for some
58 "___ moved on"

Answer on page 109.

Bill Collection

by Brendan Emmett Quigley

ACROSS

1 Instrument for Joanna Newsom or Brandee Younger
5 Swiss mathematician Leonhard
10 Free stuff in a gift bag
14 OPEC bigwig
15 Chickpeas, in some Indian dishes
16 Nelson Muntz's catchphrase
17 Arkansas city where Bill Clinton was born
18 Bill's cat when he was in the White House
19 "It depends on what the meaning of the word ___"
20. Post–Super Bowl immersion
22 Fugazi frontman MacKaye
24 Bill's White House intern Lewinsky
25 Bill's Supreme Court nominee Ruth Bader ___
30 Like one-star reviews
32 Old Testament prophet
33 Duolingo mascot
36 Seaport in France's Normandy region
38 Annoying little flaws
39 Bill's daughter
41 Hall whose June 3, 1992, show featured Bill playing 60-Down
43 Parting line
44 Become suddenly angry toward
46 Cohere, as a team
47 Like something kinda sorta wrong
49 Rockets may be sent to other cities with them
51 Fleetwood Mac song that was Bill's campaign theme
53 "I didn't ___ it, and I never tried it again" (Bill's claim about marijuana)

57 Very tiny
58 Misbehaved a bit
59 Site of Middle East accords overseen by Bill
62 Bill's nickname
65 Al who was Bill's running mate
66 Criminals' hideout
67 Beginning
68 Award for "Hedwig and the Angry Inch" in 1998
69 Chopped down
70 Creature that Marlin and Dory are briefly swallowed by, in "Finding Nemo"
71 Pirouetting points

DOWN

1 Pronouns in some bios
2 13-Down station with a torch in its logo
3 Become edible
4 Action before an auction
5 Feelings of euphoria
6 "This … isn't going great"
7 Tone-___
8 Bugler in a herd
9 Frankincense or myrrh
10 Tibia
11 "It ___ a Good Day" (1992 Ice Cube hit)
12 Tuna in some sushi
13 See 2-Down
21 Pepcid quells them
23 Burning reminder
25 "Everybody in Leather" sloganeer in the '90s
26 Roman Catholic leader, to Romans
27 Taking drugs
28 Adjust, as a halter top

29 His 16 is retired by the L.A. Lakers
31 Treating cruelly
33 The Ivy League universities, e.g.
34 Hacky Sack seller
35 Allow entrance to
37 Wipe away completely
40 Final say-so
42 Ticker repair device?
45 "Constellation According to the Laws of Chance" artist Jean
48 Florence-to-Rome dir.
50 The Four Tops' "I Almost Had Her (But ___ Away)"
52 Quarterback Tim who had a whole kneeling thing

54 Philippine ___ (dish slow-cooked in marinade)
55 Alison who won a Pulitzer Prize for her 1984 novel "Foreign Affairs"
56 Swords with two acute accents
58 Second son
59 Recife greeting
60 See 41-Across
61 Commit perjury
63 New England school that the author of this puzzle graduated from in 1996: Abbr.
64 Org. that added Archaeology and Cinematography merit badges in the '90s: Abbr.

Screen Time

BY EMET OZAR

ACROSS

1 Role for Thurman in 1998's "The Avengers"
5 Elton John and Michael Caine, for example
9 Passed with flying colors
13 One who's the opposite of licentious
14 Request
15 "Milk and Honey" poet Kaur who rose to fame on Instagram
16 Start to a waffle slogan
17 1995 MTV debut that was basically 54-Across in an RV
19 Sheltered, nautically speaking
20 "On Golden ___" (1981 film)
21 Can-do
22 Classic prank show with a 1991 reboot featuring Dom DeLuise as host
25 "Sheep be true. Baa-ram-___" ("Babe" quote)
26 Tree in the genus Quercus
27 Prior to
28 Red beryl or poudretteite, e.g.
31 One who rents
34 Like a cat's back, sometimes
36 Hot couple
38 "No Scrubs" trio
40 D.C. types
41 Changes direction
44 Dips served alongside guac, often
47 Whichever
48 "Caught you in the act!"
50 Draw
51 ___ Bo
54 MTV show that launched a genre (seen in this puzzle's shaded squares) when it debuted in 1992

57 State where the Wright brothers invented (but didn't first fly) the airplane
59 Sole
60 Part of a backsplash
61 Syndicated series that was the highest-rated court show for all of its 25-season run from 1996 to 2021
63 Chair that's carried
64 High spot
65 Those, in Spain
66 Hunts for a meal
67 Fan sound
68 Ned's lizard pet, in a 1990s Canadian animated series
69 Broadcasts

DOWN

1 Study for an attorney-to-be
2 Canadian comedy legend seen in "Waiting for Guffman" and "American Pie"
3 Sidled gradually
4 Zodiac sign between Cancer and Virgo
5 Toad the Wet ___
6 Actress Massey of old movies
7 Title for a software documentation file, often
8 Blue
9 Island mentioned in the Beach Boys' "Kokomo" (a real island, unlike Kokomo)
10 Choose from a group
11 Fencing blade
12 Bad-mouth
13 Person, ___, or thing
18 Harder to come by

20 Palm's PalmPilot and Apple's Newton, e.g.
23 Mobile platform for the iPhone
24 Time period
28 Flaming skeletal motorcyclist superhero played by Nicolas Cage (I mean, who else could it have been) in 2007
29 Fish with poor eyesight
30 Docs
32 Genre for Jimmy Eat World and Good Charlotte
33 Chicago trains
35 Accounting pro
36 Hoppy brewery offering
37 Can material
39 Agent of change
42 California resort lake
43 "Thar ___ blows!"

45 Daughter of Phil Collins whose voice was heard as a baby ape in 1999's "Tarzan"
46 Make a quilt, say
49 Excite
52 Eases, as fears
53 Paradises
54 Princess Jasmine's pet Rajah, for one
55 Provide funds for a scholarship, say
56 '90s "SNL" comic Cheri
57 "Yowza!"
58 TV cable letters
61 It might be clenched when you're tense
62 "Friends" actress Aniston, familiarly
63 Relaxation spot

Answer on page 110.

Tangled Yarn

BY Juliana Tringali Golden

ACROSS

1 Marisa of "Slums of Beverly Hills"
6 Neckwear sported by Austin Powers
11 Dial-up replacement, for short
14 Out in front
15 Island nation that joined the U.N. in 1994
16 Energy Star org. since 1992
17 Expound upon one's opinions
19 Division of labor?
20 Veggie moo ___
21 Pulitzer-winning author of "All the Light We Cannot See"
22 Weapon used by Zorro in many movies (but not "The Mask of Zorro," which featured a rapier)
23 Market craze around a certain cryptocurrency
26 Like a sandal
29 Cash for crossing
30 R&B singer ___ Lisa
31 Ray of "Twin Peaks"
32 Spots with frogs saying "Bud," "Weis," and "Er," for example
35 "That will never happen on my watch!"
40 Org. offering e-filing nationwide since 1990
41 "___ a Little Prayer" (musical number in "My Best Friend's Wedding")
42 ___-weeny (itty-bitty)
43 Japanese noodle
44 1999: California becomes the first state to recognize rights for ___ couples
47 Faint zestiness

51 Kate, to Luc in "French Kiss"
52 Radiates, like light from a fiber-optic lamp
53 Focus of the Human Genome Project
56 Charge of the state?
57 Groundbreaking 1994 film with a non-linear narrative (and a hint to the shaded squares in this puzzle's theme entries)
60 Sense of self
61 Prepare to be knighted
62 Smallest amount
63 Digs for a dragon
64 Move sneakily
65 Rapper buried in a gold casket in 1995

DOWN

1 Army bugle call
2 "Call on me! Call on me!"
3 Start ___ (Windows 95 feature)
4 Have a Hot Pocket
5 [Dusts off hands]
6 Each
7 Iliac intro
8 Brand that sponsored a "special allergy issue" of DC's Looney Tunes comic in 1998
9 Ingredient in Pop-Tarts Crunch cereal
10 "NewsRadio" night on NBC, for most episodes (they kept moving it)
11 T-shirt style with a plunging neckline
12 Rampage
13 Ale alternative

18 Publicación de Instagram
22 Slippery swimmer
23 ___ B'rith (anti-bigotry organization)
24 Down some Dunkaroos
25 Run away
26 All: Prefix
27 Far from outstanding, on a report card
28 Talking trees of Middle-earth
31 Path
32 Siamangs and such
33 Sup upon stuffed crust pizza
34 River to Hades
36 "___, Your Leash Is Too Long" (Magnetic Fields song)
37 "Time ___ the essence"

38 Like "Ellen" in 1998
39 Some jeans
43 Great Salt Lake native
44 Suppress
45 Introductory course for the visually creative
46 Asset for The Rock
47 Loathed
48 A sight to see
49 Dan Hedaya played him in "Dick"
50 Urge to move forward
53 Cameron of "The Mask"
54 Prone to prying
55 Poker buy-in
57 Soccer tie-breakers, for short
58 Start of a cycle?
59 AriZona beverage

Now That's What I Call Music!

BY TAYLOR JOHNSON

ACROSS

1 Pairs
5 "Hey ... over here"
9 Group with the 1999 album 36-Across
12 "Yesterday!"
13 "Ditto"
14 Vegan cookie
15 "Surely there's a chance"
18 "___ kickflip" (skate park challenge)
19 Gets up
20 "Forget about it!"
24 ___ cold brew
28 Sleet
29 Bird on the Eiffel Tower?
30 Campaigns for office
31 Tyler who's hosted "Whose Line Is It Anyway?" since 2013
34 Part of some gender-affirming care: Abbr.
35 Giant tub
36 Correspondence with the stars
38 Band with the 1991 album 48-Across
39 Freddy who played his first professional soccer game at age 14
40 Clumsy
41 Italian body of water
42 Scandinavian country whose nation animal is the moose
44 Like many a baker
47 Sign of spring?
48 Like a test-taker when the bell rings
50 Billionaire Carl with an eponymous New York stadium
52 Successor to Nintendo's GameCube
53 Cause for reconsideration
60 Artist with the 1996 album 53-Across
61 Loud, as a crowd
62 Chana masala side
63 GPS calculation
64 Message, in a way
65 Email folder

DOWN

1 Philip Banks was Carlton's, on "Fresh Prince of Bel-Air"
2 Utility
3 Bumbling sort
4 Web developers?
5 Aladdin's monkey Abu, e.g.
6 Strict
7 State of matter
8 Polly Pocket and Stretch Armstrong, for two
9 Attempt
10 Beirut's land: Abbr.
11 Iowa college
13 Where some try to beat the Heat?
14 Band with the 1994 album 15-Across
16 Ephron who directed and co-wrote "Sleepless in Seattle" and "You've Got Mail"
17 Like some boring work, perhaps
20 Band with the 1991 album 20-Across
21 Panama hats' country of origin, oddly
22 Giovanni ___, Italian physicist who discovered the effect of constricted flow on water pressure
23 Foolish

25 One living in Iran's capital
26 Absolute treasure of a person
27 Make obsolete
29 "___ see now!"
32 Little troublemaker
33 Occupied, as a desk
36 Utter debacle
37 "This is your brain. This is your brain on drugs. ___ questions?"
41 Certain skincare products
43 Rachel of 1999's "The Mummy"
45 Word before suit or couple
46 Tech that enables touchless credit card payments

48 Windy City hub
49 Remove from packaging (perhaps while making a video of the process)
51 Biology class subject: Abbr.
53 ___ Nabisco (conglomerate that separated in 1999)
54 Consume
55 Skipper's assent
56 Back muscle, briefly
57 Persian Gulf country: Abbr.
58 Outlaw
59 Acme product often employed by Wile E. Coyote

1	2	3	4		5	6	7	8		9	10	11
12				13					14			
15			16				17					
		18			19							
20	21	22			23				24		25	26	27
28						29						
30				31	32	33			34			
35			36	37					38			
39			40				41					
42		43			44	45	46					
47				48	49							
	50		51			52						
53	54	55			56			57	58	59		
60			61				62					
63			64				65					

Answer on page 111.

Pressing All the Right Buttons

BY ALEX EATON-SALNERS

ACROSS

1 '90s slang greeting
4 Bosom buds
8 Breathtaking sight
14 TWA posting: Abbr.
15 "Wyatt ___" (1994 Western biopic)
16 Weapon wielded by Leonardo (the ninja turtle with the blue bandana)
17 Horsey has-been
18 Titular TV surname that debuted in 1999
20 Not those
22 Free Software Foundation's animal mascot
23 Patronize, as a soda fountain
24 Victory sign
25 Aspirations
27 Latency problems in online games
28 Yoga exercise performed with spread legs
32 Affirmatives
33 "Be ___ that you can be" (U.S. Army slogan)
34 Titular canine in a 1997 sports comedy
38 Crow's call
39 "Chasing ___" (1997 rom-com)
40 Gp. with wands
41 Composite video connector, colloquially
42 25% off, say
44 It might be framed
45 Quick
46 Opening song of a 1994 Disney classic
49 Exactly

52 Bart, Lisa, and Maggie, e.g.
53 Charge point?
54 No Doubt's "___ on This"
56 Noisy dance style
57 Carl who won four consecutive long jump gold medals from 1984 to 1996
60 Plot part?
63 Hullabaloo
64 CNN founder Ted
65 "Whose Line ___ Anyway?"
66 Word in many German names
67 Instinctually recognizes
68 Egyptian cobras
69 Joe who won a Grammy in 1999 as part of Los Super Seven

DOWN

1 Email status
2 Jazz setting?
3 Obsession for early website owners
4 Make a public appearance
5 Online info source
6 With a mind toward the purse strings
7 Long-eared canine
8 Squeeze (out)
9 Cries about the litter?
10 Amazon, for one
11 Big name in orange soda
12 Remove, as someone's name from a Facebook photo
13 Sticks around until the end
19 "___ Shaker" (1992 Wreckx-N-Effect hit with the line "All I wanna do is zoom-a-zoom-zoom-zoom")

21 Black, Red, and Yellow, say
26 In order that one might
28 ___ Bell ("Make a run for the border" chain)
29 Meg of "Sleepless in Seattle"
30 Sega Saturn enthusiasts, say
31 Mononymous "Cheap Thrills" singer
35 Neural oscillation
36 Bay Area sch.
37 Mystery ___ (game whose 1999 version featured an "electronic talking phone" and a photo of a young Chris Evans on the box)
39 Laila ___, notable boxing debut of 1999
40 Jump a fence, perhaps

43 They speak louder than words
44 Target of a fabricated war in 1997's "Wag the Dog"
45 Penguin's hangout
47 Big bank, briefly
48 Some choice cuts
49 Contacts by SMS
50 At precisely the right time
51 Bedazzle, say
55 Branch location?
58 Fan favorite
59 Maker of the PlayStation ... whose controller sports four buttons found at the starts of 18-, 28-, 46-, and 60-Across
61 Salk and Pepper, say
62 Word with finger or toe

Answer on page 111.

Love Will Save the Day

by Annemarie Brethauer

ACROSS

1 1995 coming-of-age film "Now and ___"
5 The Concorde, e.g.
8 Monastery managers
14 Low-lying land
15 Fair-hiring inits.
16 Will Smith film inspired by Isaac Asimov stories
17 "You gotta be ___" (6th) (from the lyrics of 1994's "You Gotta Be" by Des'ree)
19 Actor Pat of 1994's "The Next Karate Kid"
20 National financial concerns
22 "You gotta be ___" (3rd)
23 "Your" of yore
24 Title acquired by Boxer and Feinstein in the '90s: Abbr.
25 Groanworthy wordplay
27 1995–2000 teen sitcom about a high school basketball team
29 Musical syllable
32 Rock formed by rapidly cooling lava
35 Conditioning component
36 "You gotta be ___" (7th)
37 Love, in Lombardy
38 "You gotta be ___" (1st)
39 Big ray
40 "You gotta be ___" (2nd)
41 Called the shots
42 Flowers that symbolized purity to the Victorians
43 Scratch (out)
44 Breach of etiquette

46 October birthstone
47 Company that opened the first megaplex in North America in 1995
48 Secretive org.
51 "You gotta be ___" (5th)
54 Championing
57 Feels warm and fuzzy about
59 "You gotta 55-Down ___" (9th)
60 Cites, with "to"
61 Chowed down
62 Swiss river
63 Blackboard item
64 "May I help you?"
65 Something the 48-Across might crack

DOWN

1 Best Buy buy
2 Secure door on a ship
3 Jane Jetson's son
4 Like many colors in 1990s designs
5 Talk show piece
6 Involved with
7 Moved at high speed
8 "We ___ to please"
9 "Running on Empty" singer Jackson ___
10 1990s Russian president Yeltsin
11 Japanese sashes
12 Lug around
13 "___ Trek: Deep Space Nine"
18 Cash register key

21 Emulated James Bond
26 One keeping a close eye on stealing, for short
27 "You gotta be ___" (4th)
28 A-Rod-for-Soriano action
29 Collette of 1994's "Muriel's Wedding"
30 Mechanical learning
31 "What a shame!"
32 1995 film filled with farm fauna
33 Berserk
34 Underfoot?
36 "You gotta be ___" (8th)
38 "Beauty and the Beast" heroine
39 Slip-up
41 Mauna ___

42 City known for its porcelain
44 Area of influence
45 Film for which Philip Seymour Hoffman won an Oscar
46 "Shrek" protagonists
48 Hunan hello
49 Edgar Bergen's Mortimer
50 Come to terms
51 Weigh station concern
52 Baltic Sea feeder
53 Tucson sch.
55 "You gotta ___ 59-Across" (9th)
56 Opposite of legato: Abbr.
58 Lithuania or Estonia in 1990 (but not 1992), e.g.: Abbr.

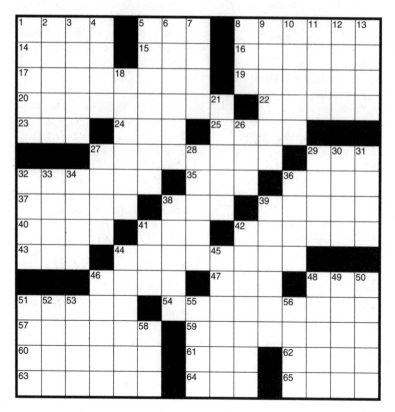

Answer on page 112.

Spikes Spikes Baby

BY KATE CHIN PARK

ACROSS

1 Layer for preventing your houndstooth skirt from sticking to your pantyhose
5 Top stories
11 Airport that became one of the busiest in the world during the dot-com boom: Abbr.
14 Rapper of the lines "Here I go, here I go, here I go again / Girls, what's my weakness?"
15 "Truly Madly ___" (1997 Savage Garden hit)
16 Billy Zane–portrayed fiancé of Rose, in "Titanic"
17 Elated beyond measure
19 Stashed
20 Surname of Lucy on "I Love Lucy"
21 Heather Locklear, Scott Wolf, and Jennifer Love Hewitt, to name three
23 Jest
24 Bails on plans, annoyingly
27 Glance at quickly
28 "Like Water ___ Chocolate"
29 Tightly packed
30 Lance who presided over the O.J. Simpson trial
32 Dubai's country: Abbr.
34 Ever, poetically
35 Artist who uses the phrase "glory hole" on a regular basis
39 Space station that explodes in "Armageddon"
41 See 1-Down
42 Munch, cutesily
43 Snack for a chipmunk
46 In the past
48 NFL team that moved from Los Angeles to St. Louis in 1995

51 Twitch mod's secret weapon?
53 Unwanted outcomes when attempting to make a cat's cradle
55 "Moonlight" is a famous one
56 ___-Kinney (band with riot grrrl origins)
58 Mike's candy pal
59 '90s hair trend ... or what 17-, 24-, 35-, and 51-Across all have?
62 To see, in Spanish
63 Targets
64 Cruel, as intentions
65 People who compile zines, for short
66 Fred to whom Koko the gorilla signed that she loved him, in a 1998 episode of his children's show
67 "I like big butts and I cannot lie / You other brothers can't ___ ..."

DOWN

1 With 41-Across, vehicle whose popularity boomed in the '90s
2 Tariffs eliminated by NAFTA, e.g.
3 Emetic once used to expel accidentally ingested poisons
4 Glide over the water, in a way
5 What a child receiving behavioral classroom management might have: Abbr.
6 Drive, à la Annika Sorenstam
7 President pro ___
8 1990s Wall St. milestone for Amazon or eBay
9 Garment similar to a cape
10 Happening together
11 Boat used by Kyle MacLachlan's "Sex and the City" character as a nickname for a certain body part (Kristin Davis's counterpart was called "Rebecca")

12 Excerpting for the purpose of parody, for example
13 Grizzled vet, so to speak
18 Thirty, in Italian
22 "Cats" initials
25 Singer of the 1999 hit "Mambo No. 5"
26 Shrinking sea that split up into two smaller seas around 1990
31 Sch. for 1997's #1 overall NFL draft pick Orlando Pace
33 Long frickin' time
35 Jokes like "You can't trust atoms. They make up everything!" and "What's orange and sounds like a parrot? A carrot!"
36 Shot in the dark

37 Did the trick
38 Wafted (from)
39 "Teardrop" band ___ Attack
40 Crestfallen summary of one's own performance
44 Nutrition fig.
45 "Getting there!"
47 Service whose features include Stolen Vehicle Assistance
49 "Murder, She Wrote" concern
50 Get involved
52 Nintendo nemesis introduced in 1992
54 "ru kidding?"
57 "___ not and say we did"
60 Texter's expression of shock
61 Opposite of NNW

Answer on page 112.

Strike a Pose

BY JASON COHEN AND ANDREA CARLA MICHAELS

ACROSS

1 Greek theater
6 Tel ___, Israel
10 Simon ___ (playground game)
14 "Chicago" murderess
15 Move, in real estate terminology
16 "Yeah, right"
17 With 40-Across and 63-Across, 1993 RuPaul hit with interjections such as "Cover girl" and "Sashay, shantay"
19 The Flintstones' purple pet
20 Kitchen gadget brand
21 Heidi Klum's runway-walking daughter
22 Did, but doesn't now
24 1990s 17-Across who was the first Black women to appear on the cover of French Vogue
27 Quinze doubled
29 The smallest wood in the golf bag?
30 William who has a state named after him
31 "The Lion King" character with three hyena henchmen
34 Item on the red side of the ledger
39 With 41-Across, 1990s 17-Across who was the face of Calvin Klein ads
40 See 17-Across
41 See 39-Across
42 Car that wasn't one of Ford's "better ideas"
44 Ran, like a tie-dye shirt in the wash
46 Scott of "Charles in Charge"
47 Game without losers

49 "Fore!" and "Duck!," e.g.
51 1990s 17-Across who, with Richard Gere, was half of People magazine's Sexiest Couple Alive in 1993
57 Remove any doubt about
58 "It's ___ her" (relationship ultimatum)
59 Band with the 1991 hit "Shiny Happy People"
62 Pringles competitor
63 See 17-Across
66 Clothes dryer accumulation
67 Massage reactions
68 Words before care or mind
69 "The Lord of the Rings" creatures
70 Western novelist Zane
71 Namesakes of a Salinger girl

DOWN

1 Words of approximation
2 Billets-___ (love letters)
3 Mathematical powers
4 180° turn, slangily
5 Dry red wine
6 Rice-___ ("The San Francisco Treat")
7 Related to Hindu scripture
8 Land in la mer
9 Library unit
10 Part of a 45
11 Play (by), as rules
12 "Papa, Can You Hear Me?" movie musical
13 Counter seat
18 "Grumpy cat" and "distracted boyfriend," for example

23 Zoomed
25 Year, in Ypres
26 "Based on ___ story"
27 I-90 in Mass., e.g.
28 Use a Kindle, say
32 Prefix with space or punk
33 EarthLink competitor
35 Smoldering coal
36 Where the top brass meets
37 "___ bigger than a breadbox?"
38 General ___ chicken
43 About 5.88 trillion miles: Abbr.
45 "The English Patient" actor Willem

48 Swelling reducer
50 Singer Morgan with the 1991 country hit "Except for Monday"
51 Yo-Yo strings?
52 "... the bombs bursting ___"
53 "No Strings Attached" pop group
54 Cleans off with a dry cloth
55 "I ___ night" (quote from "Batman: The Animated Series")
56 Betsy ___ (collectible doll)
60 Eagle along the shore
61 NYSE and Nasdaq, e.g.
64 Organ with a hammer inside
65 Part of wpm: Abbr.

Answer on page 113.

The One About...

BY LAURA BRAUNSTEIN

ACROSS

1 Colleague of La Forge and Troi
5 Asparagus stalk
10 Wine's scent
14 Brother of Cain
15 Land in Lyon
16 "What's the big ___?"
17 Roman war god
18 "Groundhog Day" director Harold
19 Following
20 Guest star of "The One About the Teenager Who Won Nine Grand Slams"?
23 Gibbon or bonobo, e.g.
24 Band that had a "Part II" offshoot without Jeff Lynne in the '90s
25 "Don't drink and ___!" (math pun)
29 Head
34 Egg source, in mammals
35 "___ About You" (sitcom on which Lisa Kudrow played the twin sister of her "Friends" character)
38 Water filter brand
39 Media company founded in 1994
40 "Wonderwall" band
42 When doubled, a Hawaiian fish
43 Archaic verb ending
44 Raises, as a car with a flat
46 Denials
47 Maker of the Pump athletic shoe
49 Turn of ___ (wording choice)
51 Fib
52 Bit of cribbage gear
55 "___ Bodies, ___selves" (groundbreaking health manual)
56 Fit of pique
58 ___Clean stain remover
59 Sherlock Holmes's cinematic sister
62 Suitor
63 Beach initials
64 Established
65 Like the Copacabana scene in "GoodFellas"

67 Dangerous flies
69 Type of cell division
71 Guest star of "The One About Philip Marlowe's Creator"?
79 "Insane in the ___" (1993 Cypress Hill song)
80 Cry of surprise
81 "Straight ___ Compton" (2015 biopic)
82 Crystal-filled stone
83 M-Q link
84 Verbose

DOWN

1 Obstruct
2 Lawyers' org.
3 Semester or trimester, e.g.
4 As well
5 Roadway marker
6 "See ya!"
7 Bombeck who wrote "Motherhood: The Second Oldest Profession"
8 Get up
9 Operate a thrift shop, say
10 Seven of ___ ("Star Trek" role for Jeri Ryan)
11 Praiseful works
12 "___ and the City"
13 "Go ___ Worms!" ("Goosebumps" book)
21 Word before blue or bean
22 "Stay (I Missed You)" singer Lisa
25 Delaware's capital
26 Party-planning platform founded in 1998
27 Guest star of "The One About the Boho-Chic Designer"?
28 Fury
30 River's division
31 Guest star of "The One About the Motown Diva"?
32 Belief system
33 Salary bump

35 Word after Big or Fleetwood
36 Inquire
37 Put down
40 "Gospel ___" (1997 Sinéad O'Connor EP)
41 "How's it hangin'?"
44 Guest star of "The One About the Godfather of American Punk"?
45 Guest star of "The One About the Blues Singer Best Known for 'Poetry Man'"?
48 French operatic composer Georges
50 Assail
52 Neptune's Greek counterpart
53 "Sell by" info: Abbr.
54 "Exit Through the ___" (2010 Banksy film)

56 "___ snaps up!" (positive review from an "In Living Color" sketch)
57 Charged atom
60 Director Spike or Ang
61 Spots
66 Guy in a Barbie queue?
68 One-named "Chandelier" singer
70 Tres plus cinco
71 "Notorious" SCOTUS justice
72 Equal
73 Eight-time NBA All-Star Ming
74 Central
75 Hall & Oates or Insane Clown Posse, e.g.
76 Copier setting: Abbr.
77 JFK listing
78 Amy of Indigo Girls

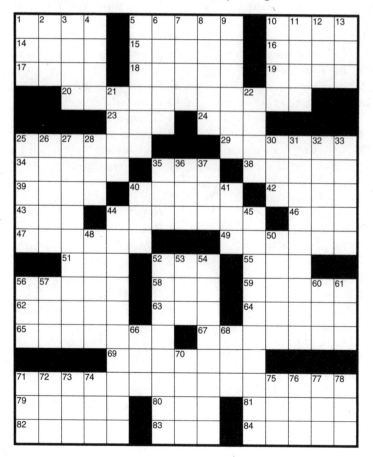

Answer on page 113.

Solving the Night Away

BY KAREN LURIE

ACROSS

1 Kick back
5 "Srsly?!"
8 Manage somehow
12 Get knocked down
14 Cannes king
15 Passionate
16 Sprain treatment
17 1997 Booker Prize winner "The ___ of Small Things"
18 Clarinet necessity
19 Loooong time
20 Cartoon enemies in perpetuity
23 "The Crow" co-star ___ Ling
25 Not unless
26 Light wind coming toward the shore
29 Impedes, with "up"
32 "A ___'s a ___, no matter how small" ("Horton Hears a Who!" assertion)
33 Fireplace leftover
35 "Get off my ___!"
37 Coffee table book subject
38 "This is delicious" onomatopoeia
40 Fishy, for short
42 Essential
43 Omani money
45 Member of the fam
47 Binges
49 Site founded as AuctionWeb in 1995
51 Injury indicated by two puncture wounds
53 Exploit a situation
55 Quibble
56 1997 Chumbawamba song for which 20-Across could be the "whiskey drink," 26-Across could be the "vodka drink," and 51-Across could be both the "lager drink" and "cider drink"
60 Scold
63 Cookie with a cereal that was introduced in 1997
64 GPS display
65 Pleats ___ (1993 Issey Miyake collection)
67 Summer quenchers
68 Function
69 Get up again
70 Con
71 High degree
72 Speechify in an unhinged fashion

DOWN

1 Bananas
2 Something you have to settle
3 Patrol car alert: Abbr.
4 Hair-straightening tool
5 Gauzy material
6 Like an especially dark night
7 Euphoric
8 "Watch your back!"
9 "I'm done," on a walkie-talkie
10 Fishing spot
11 Whirlpool
12 ___-dye (retro trend of the '90s)

13 Vanity
21 Springfield's Szyslak
22 Folk dance
24 Core muscles
26 Practice like Evander Holyfield
27 Uncanny
28 Only chimp to orbit the Earth
30 Throw money, say
31 "Awesome!"
34 Corn cover
36 Wall Street letters
39 Patchwork
41 Only original Ghostbuster in 1997's "Extreme Ghostbusters"
44 Some find it intolerable
46 Made small cuts
48 Baseball stat
50 Affirmative heard in 1996's "Fargo"
52 "Not a Pretty Girl" singer DiFranco
54 Recap
56 Protagonist of the Nintendo game "Wario's Woods"
57 Pakistan's lingua franca
58 Doubled, it precedes "Who got the keys to the Jeep?"
59 "World Cafe" airer
61 Type of D.A.
62 "Golly!"
66 Clinton's covered most of the '90s

Answer on page 114.

Millennium Approaches

BY ENRIQUE HENESTROZA ANGUIANO

ACROSS

1 Channel that premiered "TRL" in 1998
4 Handlebar cover
8 Chiapas or Oaxaca, e.g.
14 Yellowfin tuna
15 Singer/activist Horne
16 Chimed in
17 Pigs-in-a-blanket dressing?
19 Ouija board session
20 Raise with pulleys
21 Ram sign
22 Actress who played Anna Madrigal on 1993's LGBT-oriented "Tales of the City"
26 Hospital area with IVs
27 Japanese currency
28 "The Baby-Sitters Club" writer ___ M. Martin
29 ___ loss for words
30 Spiced tea
32 Proud playground retort
34 Trivia video game series that debuted in 1995 with a memorable theme song for question 4 ("The Question That Cares")
41 Word after soap or space
42 Fruit infused in gin
43 Pokémon trainer Ketchum
46 "___ vez más" ("once more")
47 Indulgent spree
50 Multiple-era stretch
51 He directed then-married Cruise and Kidman in 1999's "Eyes Wide Shut"

55 "No ___ Bob!"
56 Bit of tomfoolery
57 Connective tissue that extends from hip to knee, familiarly
59 Comedic battle that gets sticky?
63 Spirit in a Penicillin
64 LiveJournal entry
65 Concerning type of bug in the late '90s ... or what three answers in this puzzle each contain
66 In the ___ of passion
67 Creative fields
68 ___ point (a cow's opinion, per Joey on "Friends")

DOWN

1 Wrestling surface
2 Nonetheless, briefly
3 Contend (for)
4 Down in the dumps
5 "Baking With Julia" bit
6 Finishes, as a tattoo
7 Lasagna divider
8 Canon camera model
9 Alternative to "forever hold your peace"
10 Accessory for Brandy in 1997's "Cinderella"
11 LPGA legend Sörenstam
12 Duplicity
13 City in Ukraine or Texas
18 A bit of a wallflower
22 Calle ___ (historic Miami street)

23 Hawaiian feast
24 "I'm impressed!"
25 Biblical preposition
26 Far from friendly
31 Words pronounced many times in 1994's "Four Weddings and a Funeral"
32 Alias letters
33 IHOP beverages
35 "___! You own everything!": "Paris Is Burning"
36 Little chiquillo
37 Sloppy joe and fruit cocktail holder, maybe
38 Ewan's Obi-Wan predecessor
39 Grill up some Boca Burgers, say

40 2023 role for Ryan Gosling, Simu Liu, and Ncuti Gatwa, among others
43 Pippen-to-Jordan scoring play
44 Part of a softball
45 Place to drop anchor
47 Donkey Kong's son
48 Marketing experiment comparing two variants
49 Small-scale swindles
52 "Wowee zowee!"
53 Phi Beta ___
54 Here, in Honfleur
58 MLB players who only bat
60 Dodgeball venue at school
61 Water, molecularly
62 Ref's bout-ending decision

Answer on page 114.

"1990s Game Shows for $200, Alex"

by Trip Payne

ACROSS

1 Sounds like a banshee
6 Women, to a cowpoke
10 1996 AL MVP runner-up, for short
14 Time unit?
15 Number that might include a high C
16 Butterfly's chrysalis, for example
17 1990s MTV game show where a Picker might award a Golden Ticket to some in the Dating Pool
19 Black cloud, perhaps
20 O.J.'s notable houseguest
21 ___-com ("You've Got Mail," say)
22 Bring in
24 Orange County city
27 "The Facts of Life" star Charlotte
28 Birthplace of St. Francis
31 Chatty pet
33 Game where you collect three cards at a time
34 Cold War defense alliance: Abbr.
37 Result of poor insulation, perhaps
40 Eaglet's birthplace
42 "Sheesh!"
43 Flight attendant's beat
44 Focus (heh) of the "Dark Side of the Moon" album cover
45 Score for a newborn
47 It's charged
48 The "P" of PBR

50 ___ at windmills (made like Don Quixote)
52 Slitherer near the Nile
54 Character who first appeared in Action Comics #1
57 Garlic units
59 Vacuum's lack
60 Omani or Yemeni, typically
64 Gross receipts
65 1990s syndicated game show that was super-similar to "Win, Lose, or Draw"
68 Like only one prime
69 It could measure 66 feet by 660 feet
70 Barrier mentioned in the song "American Pie"
71 "Jurassic Park" actress Laura
72 Pudu or muntjac, for example
73 Make oneself presentable

DOWN

1 Former rival of Tide
2 It's covered by 11 time zones
3 Word of denial
4 Actor whose final film appearance was in "Plan 9 From Outer Space"
5 Fleur de ___ (fancy seasoning)
6 Portrayer of Wonder Woman
7 Coffeeshop emanation
8 Actress Lucy who's mentioned in the song "Hey Ya!"
9 Glossy and smooth

10 Per person
11 1990s VH1 game show with a Scandalation Instant Reflex round
12 Beethoven created one
13 He's nicknamed "il Sommo Poeta"
18 "Rubber Duckie" singer
23 Most-spoken language on Earth
25 Verb for the Avengers
26 ___ Us (game inspired by Mafia)
28 Immediately if not sooner
29 Dealer in futures?
30 1990s USA game show where losers would end up in their underwear
32 MSNBC host Melber
35 Vintage violin
36 Create Morse code, perhaps
38 Large mass of ice

39 Have a leaning
41 "This ___ rip-off!"
46 Maker of the 2600 and 5200 consoles
49 Scouring item
51 One-point shot in horseshoes
52 Did something
53 Grace Jones's "___ to the Rhythm"
55 "___ bleu!"
56 Carafe amount
58 Type of diagram with multiple circles
61 "The best film of the year!," for example
62 Savage deity
63 Top seeds may receive them
66 Ephemeral sculpting medium
67 Like nonagenarians, say

Answer on page 115.

Move With Me

by Alex Eaton-Salners

ACROSS

1 Suits are their strong suit
7 Pipe blockage
11 Writes an app, say
16 Stone of "Basic Instinct"
17 ___! Cherry-O (classic board game)
18 Poised to spring into action
19 Tropical houseplants
21 Concrete-strengthening rod
22 More like a fox
23 Toy that's always making a comeback?
25 Simile center
26 HR rep on "The Office"
29 Bicycle wheel?
31 Chatroom chuckle
32 Patch (up)
33 "Wonder" garment in a famous 1994 ad campaign featuring Eva Herzigova
34 Disrespects by ignoring
37 Chief god in the Rig-Veda
39 December 31, 1999, say
40 Jam container
41 Boosts on social media
44 Looking glass?
46 Novelist's concern
50 Setting for a musical hit?
52 Floral fruit used in teas
54 In ___ (dancing in perfect lock step with all the other members of one's boy band, say)
55 Tamagotchi is a proper one
57 Mark with grooves
58 Lummox
60 Portable crash site?
62 Hollywood's second tier
63 Seasonal green drink
69 Ashley, to Mary-Kate
70 Greedily monopolize
71 Pool accessory
72 ___ Gagarin, first person in space
73 Chromosome component
74 Terminal fig.
75 The titular dinosaur in Pixar's "The Good Dinosaur"
77 "Abort, ___, Fail?"
79 Sized up, before a heist
81 '90s dance craze ... whose steps are seen at the ends of 19-, 34-, 50-, 52-, and 63-Across
86 Wedding walkway
87 "The Bridges of Madison County" state
88 Kind of energy
89 Some salon services
90 2022 Olympic figure skating gold medalist Nathan
91 Outcome

DOWN

1 Nile biter
2 Greek letter after pi
3 Mouse pad, essentially
4 Pretentiously bohemian
5 Gallagher of Oasis (the one who wrote most of the songs)
6 ___ Girls ("Closer to Fine" duo)
7 Indicate with mime, in a game
8 Wee wee?
9 "Great Scott!"
10 Emulate Geri Halliwell in 1999
11 "Loveline" co-host Adam
12 "Huzzah!"
13 Lower in value, as currency
14 Writer's block?
15 Milkshake sippers
20 Spa treatment
24 "That's a joke, right?"
26 "Grease" gang named after a sporty Ford
27 Cantankerous

28 Groanworthy crossword clue, perhaps
30 Invite letters
34 Quarters, say
35 Exercise the ears
36 Late-'90s regular on "The Oprah Winfrey Show"
38 "Four Weddings and a Funeral" or "There's Something About Mary," say
42 "Roger that!"
43 ___ Paulo, Brazil
45 Graphing calculator figs.
47 Act as a go-between
48 Chooses to be marketed to, say
49 Fly around Africa?
51 Launchpad McQuack, for one
53 Kathryn of "Oz"
56 Offensively inquisitive

59 Places to play Street Fighter II or Crazy Taxi
61 Uma of "Pulp Fiction"
63 Tom's mate (or a DC Comics villain of 1997 who had a grudge against Selina Kyle)
64 Windbags are full of it
65 U.S. Open winner in 1994 and 1999
66 Larry Bird or Paul Pierce, say
67 Demarcated space
68 Build-it-yourself auto
73 Wraps served with tzatziki
76 "Teacher! I know the answer!"
78 Give an "R" or a "G" to
80 Tree with an asymmetric ovate leaf
82 She gets sheared
83 "Move Like an ___" (Wiggles song)
84 It means nothing
85 Play part

Answer on page 115.

Clueless People

BY STELLA ZAWISTOWSKI

ACROSS

1 Good thing to have
6 Sharpen, as knives or skills
10 "No Ordinary Love" was her only Top 40 hit in the 1990s
14 Get more Sassy?
15 Black eyeliner–wearing types
16 Like a Swatch watch
18 Hamlet or Oedipus, say (Alicia Silverstone)
20 Climate pattern whose name means "the girl"
21 Maple syrup precursor
22 Hunan "how you doing?"
23 Sent to the Hill
24 Año beginning
25 Get the band together, so to speak
26 Close chum
29 Classical works for small groups (Elisa Donovan)
34 Neighborhoods with lots of Spanish speakers
36 www.aclu.___
37 Follower of the Way of the Guru
38 Red ___ (famed fighter of oil fires)
39 Site where you can book a contractor
40 Molecule with "messenger" and "transfer" varieties
41 Novelty officewear for Weird Al fans, perhaps (Stacey Dash)
47 Wilton Guerrero was caught using a corked one in 1997
48 Close relative of jealousy
49 Birds' body parts where food is stored
50 Word that might precede bad news
52 "All That ___ Wants" (Ace of Base hit)
53 Either of two Spice Girls
55 Brand that sells cheap flights (Brittany Murphy)
59 Ganja

60 "Please Don't Go ___" (plea from New Kids on the Block)
61 Singer Day who played Billie Holiday
63 "The Amy Fisher Story" was one
66 Windows precursor
67 Roadie's load
70 Utter bliss
71 Rich, gem-inspired colors (Jeremy Sisto)
73 On the wrong path
74 ___'s Daily Roast (coffee chain)
75 God of thunder, in Hindu mythology
76 Ancient pyramid builders
77 Ten Forward and Quark's, in the "Star Trek" universe
78 Button on a Super Nintendo console

DOWN

1 The "A" in STEAM
2 "Que ___, ___" ("What will be, will be")
3 How to follow up a bend, per Elle Woods
4 Meas. of brain activity
5 String for trussing a turkey
6 Villainous chuckles
7 Golfer Mark who won the Masters and the Open in 1998
8 "Sorry, we're filled to capacity!"
9 Spanish "that"
10 Part of a sung mass whose name means "holy"
11 Came down to the ground
12 Ready to eat
13 Melodramatic exclamation
16 Medically oversensitive
17 Fashion designer Khan
19 Number between cuatro and seis
23 Come into view
26 Reason for booing a ref

27 Repeating design in mathematics
28 Opposite of "caliente"
30 German city where Beethoven was born
31 Fashion designer Christian
32 "Told you so!"
33 Gliding step in ballet
34 "___ Black Sheep" (nursery rhyme)
35 Like some discounted mdse.
39 One or more
42 Having a craving for
43 Take a deep breath
44 Appliance on "The Great British Bake Off"
45 Potassium chloride, to a chemist
46 One of many set by Kevin McAllister in "Home Alone"
51 Classical guitarist Andrés

53 Trash heaps studied by archaeologists
54 Weasley family owl in the Potterverse
56 Donated
57 Tia's sis on "Sister, Sister"
58 It's given in the form of a question on "Jeopardy!"
62 Up and moving
63 Possible pronoun choice for a non-binary person
64 Wang who dressed Nancy Kerrigan in the 1990s
65 "Real Love" singer ___ J. Blige
67 No ifs, ___, or buts
68 Nothing more than
69 Exam with a high score of 1520
71 Butcher, baker, or candlestick maker
72 Half and half?

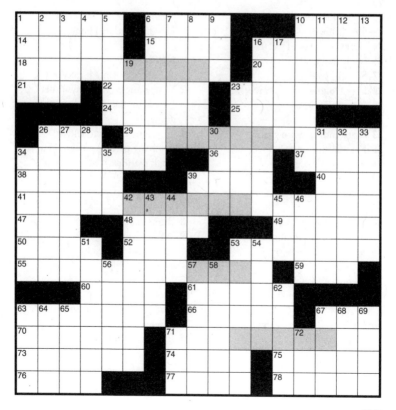

Answer on page 116.

Finger-Lickin' Good

BY SID SIVAKUMAR

ACROSS

1 French ___ ('90s manicure trend)
5 Slideshow-ready Excel output
10 Insult
13 Strike down, biblically
15 Food processor setting
16 Animal that sounds like you?
17 More up to the task
18 "Touched by an ___" (TV drama whose main character delivers messages from God to people)
19 Kind of office transmission ubiquitous in the '90s
20 Copy, for short
22 Aquatic mammals featured in the film "Flipper"
24 Greek goddess of the dawn
25 Beginnings
27 Solemn vow
28 Play Double Dutch at recess, say
30 Interesting in trying
32 Remain unsettled
33 Outstanding exam grade
35 Flannel shirt, e.g.
36 Smartphone installs
39 R&B legend Redding
41 Mixed martial arts org. founded in 1993
44 Summer ___ (sleepaway destinations for kids)
46 Smoothie bowl berry
50 Exactly on time
52 Chopper's touchdown site
55 Box ___ (inexpensive room coolers)
56 Hades and Pluto's Egyptian counterpart

58 Hindu mantra syllables
59 Novelty candy items worn on fingers ... as illustrated by the circled letters in this puzzle
61 Early-age Lego brick brand
63 Love lines?
64 Jazz supporter, probably
66 Assert
68 Advisory gp. to the president
69 Stopwatch readouts
70 Knightley who played Queen Amidala's body double in "The Phantom Menace"
71 Rug rat
72 "Selma" actress Thompson
73 Doodled with gel pens, say

DOWN

1 Airport screening letters
2 "There's nothing in my wallet"
3 Enters the Honda Odyssey as a group, say
4 ___ aerobics (exercise fad involving getting on and off a small platform)
5 H.S. student's stat
6 Be felt very strongly
7 Jargon
8 Burns rubber
9 "Would you like ___?" (annoying offer from Microsoft's virtual assistant Clippy)
10 Like a rebel
11 "Let me try!"
12 Place to make some adult purchases
14 Blue Screen of Death, e.g.

21 "Rising" singer Yoko
23 Groundbreaking tool?
24 Mentalist's alleged ability, for short
26 Muscle twitch
29 Device such as a BlackBerry
31 Trident-shaped letter
34 Player who experiences a "fatality" in Mortal Kombat
37 Illicit hallucinogen, briefly
38 Keister
40 Maple syrup source
41 At the outset
42 "Yep, sorry to say"
43 Hook up, as with LAN cables
45 Scams by email

47 Welcome forecast on a summer day
48 Fancy-sounding cupboard for clothing
49 "___ morphin' time!" ("Power Rangers" catchphrase)
51 Umami-imparting flavor additive: Abbr.
53 Mason jar topper
54 "My skills are total garbage"
57 Bombards with AIM messages, say
60 Shot on a mini-golf course
62 Begged
65 U.S. intelligence org.
67 Gaping mouth

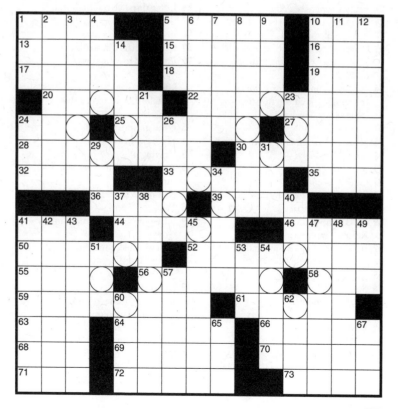

Answer on page 116.

The Crane-Beau Connection

BY TONY ORBACH

ACROSS

1 Like a windbag
6 Seldom-used first name of Jerry's neighbor on "Seinfeld"
11 ___ tzu (mop-shaped dog)
15 Sharp
16 Churchill's supporters
17 Man of Milano
18 "Cheers" actress who revived her role as 49-Across's ex-wife, Lilith Sternin
20 Socks
21 Salinger title character
22 Middle: Prefix
23 Takes up the challenge
25 Saudi, e.g.
27 Printer paper size: Abbr.
29 Crop up
30 Leave a blemish on
32 "Married to the Mob" actress who played a boss (and romantic interest) of 49-Across
36 "___ Baba and the forty thieves" (repeated lyric in the Beastie Boys' "Rhymin & Stealin")
37 Gratis
38 "Go ___ Watchman" (Harper Lee novel)
39 Jeans material
41 Gallery display
43 Sneeze with a big wind-up
48 Chevy subcompact
49 ___ Crane (Longtime role for Kelsey Grammer)
52 Italian wedding or French onion
53 Smoky liquor from Mexico
55 "___ luck?"
56 Sad song
57 Loch ___ monster
60 Give up
62 Kraken org.
63 "Malcolm in the Middle" actress who played a cop that 49-Across was attracted to (but who ended up dating 49-Across's dad)

68 Some football linemen: Abbr.
69 "The ___ Suspects" (1995 movie with a police lineup on the poster)
70 Battery type
71 Healthcare prefix
73 Exam halfway through a course
75 Caramel candy brand
78 Stone or Watson
81 Senate aide
82 "NYPD Blue" actress who played an ex-lawyer-turned-pastry-chef who dates 49-Across
85 Longtime Disney CEO Bob
86 Long-distance traveler's woe
87 Bit the dust
88 Prying
89 Cosmetician Elizabeth
90 Precursor to Windows

DOWN

1 Buffalo Bills receiver Davis
2 Whizzes
3 U-boats, for instance
4 Have the helm
5 Craving
6 Animals seen in many "Far Side" cartoons
7 Baltimore baseball player
8 "Yes, ___!"
9 Silly phrase of agreement in a crowd
10 Fed. workplace watchdog
11 Outback or Forester
12 ___ & the Blowfish
13 Mischievous
14 Youth ___ (low-cost travel accommodation option)
16 Mon. follower
19 Glowing remnant
24 "Buffy the Vampire Slayer" star ___ Michelle Gellar
26 Radio toggle

28 NFL scores
30 "___ Secretary" (Téa Leoni show that co-starred 18-Across)
31 Advil rival
33 Posterior
34 Actor Michael of "Superbad"
35 Celeb
40 Summer Games gp.
42 Screening org.
44 CBS franchise encompassing five series
45 Like the glasses worn by Weezer's Rivers Cuomo
46 Should, with "to"
47 Cars that sound like jewels
49 Red Hot Chili Peppers bass player seen in "The Big Lebowski"
50 Pre-Columbian Peruvian
51 Observer
54 Leg joint
56 Feint on the ice

58 One sending an email like "We have noticed an attempt to log into your account, please confirm your password at bonkofmerica.com or your account will be deleted"
59 "Kill Bill" singer
61 Evil spirit
63 Eschew the pool stairs, perhaps
64 Sharp Italian cheese
65 Prods with an elbow
66 Diner
67 Countertop material
72 Specifics, informally
74 Indian king
76 Port of Algeria
77 ___ lamp ("major award" in "A Christmas Story")
79 Springtime month in Lisbon
80 Kitchen pests
83 Since Jan. 1
84 '60s war zone, briefly

Answer on page 117.

Everyone's a Critic

BY BRENDAN EMMETT QUIGLEY

ACROSS

1 1990 hit by Tesla
6 Bulls ran wild through it in the '90s: Abbr.
9 ___ Fresh (Tex-Mex chain)
13 City where Berkshire Hathaway is headquartered
14 Feel sick
15 "It's been ___"
16 Singer that made Beavis realize, "This guy does everything by himself"
18 Band that made Butt-head comment, "These guys are pretty cool for a bunch of mimes"
19 Show whose first and last guest hosts of the '90s were Ed O'Neill and Danny DeVito
20 Climatology, e.g.: Abbr.
21 On a razor's edge
22 Band that made Butt-head ask, "Is this the Partridge Family?"
25 Comprehend
26 ___ Nui (Easter Island)
29 Water wings filler
30 Name on the range
32 "Real Housewives" star Kirschenheiter
33 Bartender who gets frequent prank phone calls
36 Singer that made Butt-head say, "This is that guy with all those last names"
39 Artifact in the Well of Souls
40 Bumbling dummkopfs
41 Number of World Series won by the Yankees in the '90s
42 Org. in charge of enforcing 1990's Pollution Prevention Act
43 Accutane treats it

44 Little dog, for short
47 Band that made Beavis ask, "Hey Butt-head, remember when these guys were cool?," to which Butt-head replied, "Uhhh ... No."
51 Sweet bouquet
53 Sorority letter
54 Not so many
57 Band that made Butt-head comment, "These guys are from, like, Austria or something"
58 Band that made Butt-head say, "These guys are pretty cool, even though they're 60," while Beavis replied "Yeah, that one guy's 69"
61 Dark film genre
62 "I'm Audi 5000"
63 Fit to be tied
64 Picture in an IKEA manual, e.g.
65 Follow a thread?
66 Industry giant

DOWN

1 Has a good cry
2 "Sign me up"
3 Brazen boldness
4 Penguins' gp.
5 Approval
6 Rock bottom
7 Spot for pronouns
8 ___ Saints (British girl group with the 1997 hit "Never Ever")
9 Smoke some weed
10 Getting on in years
11 TV cook (of a sort) Pinkman
12 Thing in the plus column
17 Post-ER location
21 Leader you can't reason with
22 Wenner who co-founded the Rock and Roll Hall of Fame

23 Mani-pedi targets
24 "___ Kleine Middle Klasse Music" (Rutles song from 1996's "Archaeology")
26 South Asian king
27 Telenovela theme
28 "___ yah cah in Hahvahd Yahd"
31 One-celled organism
32 Gather, as bits of information
33 Summers who hosted "Double Dare"
34 A broken mirror is a bad one
35 Electrified Olympic equipment
37 Show that debuts new products
38 Spicy cuppa
44 Ibuprofen targets

45 "Changed my mind"
46 "You got ___, kid!"
48 Eddie Bauer rival
49 "Well, well, well, look at this"
50 Stop in on
52 Number causing some sticker shock, for short
54 21-Down's decree
55 Candy in the Wonder Woman universe
56 "My schedule's wide open"
58 Six-pack muscles
59 ___ of Horus (option when choosing "Only Connect" questions)
60 Test with magnets: Abbr.

Get Psyched

BY PAOLO PASCO

ACROSS

1 Month abbr. that becomes a different month abbr. when you shift every letter back two places in the alphabet
4 Jumping ability, casually
8 Richie who played with the Commodores
14 Oom-___ (tuba onomatopoeia)
15 "That's ... incorrect"
16 Who Jimmy Dugan says looks like "a penis with a little hat on," in "A League of Their Own"
17 Bird that Steve Irwin once caught with his bare hands, according to legend
18 Tom Selleck series ... psych! It's actually wine from a condom manufacturer
20 Marvel star Jeremy
22 "Noted"
23 "I had to haul ___ to the kitchen, redistribute the food, squish in extra place settings, but by the end of the day, it was, like, the more the merrier!" ("Clueless" quote)
24 Cousin of a birch tree
25 Features of Mr. Sketch markers
27 With 38- and 48-Across, O. Henry short story ... psych! It's a donation from the namesake of a "line" in World War II!
29 Tatooine has two
31 British noble
32 Tamblyn who played Dr. Jacoby on "Twin Peaks"
35 6, in Spanish
37 "The license plate said FRESH and it had ___ in the mirror" (statement about the cab that took Will to Bel-Air)
38 See 27-Across
40 "___ Prohibido" (1994 Selena album)
42 Piece of equipment in a pool room or a torture chamber

44 Hanging feature of some safari hats
45 Nut in 52-Down, once
46 Roof option for some old cars
48 See 27-Across
50 Comfort
53 Comforts, maybe
54 Pikachu's owner
57 Letter before Lima, in the NATO phonetic alphabet
58 "Door's wide open for us"
59 Cereal brand ... psych! It's a Boy Scout's most prized rope trick
62 Main squeeze, nowadays
63 Big gumbo vessel
64 Awards show achievement completed posthumously by Audrey Hepburn in 1994
65 Turn-___ (subject of some video dating profiles)
66 ___ COIN (arcade machine message)
67 Meh
68 Exclamation at the end of a sarcastic sentence ... and at the end of this puzzle's theme entries

DOWN

1 Ran
2 Coat material collected from Bactrians
3 "Them Changes" musician whose name was inspired by a feline cartoon series
4 Funny bones, scientifically
5 "Juice" star Epps
6 .gif alternative
7 "Adventures of ___ the Hedgehog" (1993 cartoon that ran for one 65-episode-long season)
8 Lightbulb-measuring units
9 Motivating force
10 Nail polish brand with color names like "Over the Taupe" and "Aurora Berry-alis"

11 Dr. Albright's assistant, on "3rd Rock from the Sun"
12 God who'd love to talk about sex
13 "___ Talk About Sex"
19 Guns N' Roses' 1991 albums "___ Your Illusion I" and "___ Your Illusion II"
21 Fails to care for, as one's Tamagotchi
25 Things
26 Better at playing hide and seek, maybe
28 To and ___
30 Duran Duran's lead singer
33 "What's Love Got to Do With It" setting, for short
34 Feeling after remembering that time you tried to rock a soul patch, maybe
36 What many sonatas are written for
39 Government org. that probably didn't love all the hairspray that people used in the '90s
41 "Sty" alternative, in terms of "names for a messy room"
43 More like the Addams Family (according to their theme song)
47 Like movable types?
49 Location in a 1969 hit for Elvis
51 "___ That" (show featuring the recurring characters Repairman-man-man-man and Pierre Escargot)
52 Certain soda fountain orders
54 Big name in sparkling wine
55 Did pirouettes, say
56 Last word in the "she series" of pronouns
58 Plays "In Your Eyes" from a boombox for, maybe
60 Letter before dee
61 Gp. like HelpAge International or BRAC

You Oughta Know

by Taylor Johnson

ACROSS

1 First name in '90s West Coast hip-hop
6 Zapped, as an unwanted tattoo
11 Feeling that everyone's having fun without you, initially
15 Roulette bets
16 Candy heart inscription
17 Regretted
18 Singer of 66-Across who portrayed God in the 1999 comedy "Dogma"
21 Ink spots?
22 Snarky chuckle
23 Jazz legend Waters
24 Genre for Sunny Day Real Estate and American Football
25 Steadfast
27 Revises
30 One receiving compensation
32 "Get ___ town!"
35 Kilmer of 1995's "Batman Forever" and "Heat"
36 Achieve bronze?
37 Israeli desert
38 One who's next in line for the throne
39 Ranch ingredient
41 "Leggo my ___!"
43 Simple sammies
46 Rise up
49 Dated
51 Sailor's assent
52 Former U.S. Secretary of State and Peace Nobelist Root
53 Notify
55 Hot's partner
57 Blue toon

59 ___ Kippur
61 Like "Goosebumps" stories
64 She, in Rio
65 Boo-boo
66 1995 studio album by by 18-Across, and what you'll find four times in this grid, literally?
70 Gymnast Korbut called "the Sparrow from Minsk"
71 Boxer De La Hoya who won gold in Barcelona in 1992
72 Like notebook paper
73 Upright instrument
74 Eric Clapton hit that charted a second time in its "MTV Unplugged" version
75 Connects

DOWN

1 Entice
2 Certain salon fixture
3 Thick outerwear
4 St. ___ Bay, Jamaica
5 Long-running TV procedural
6 Like pico de gallo or guacamole, maybe
7 Classic Hawaiian folk song
8 Big ___ (California coastal region)
9 Singer Sands
10 Untouched book collection?
11 Let loose
12 Last longer than, say
13 ___ Gala
14 Dedicated words
19 Word after horse or saddle
20 ___ butter (skincare product)
25 "Queen & Slim" co-screenwriter Waithe

26 Drag
28 "Clueless" transfer student who Cher decides to make over
29 Camera type: Abbr.
31 Seasonal side dish
33 Mad, with "off"
34 "Suitable for anyone tuning in" rating
37 "Me? Uh-uh"
38 Courtney Love band with the 1994 album "Live Through This"
40 Fashion monogram
42 Sport conducted in rounds
43 Scrooge exclamation
44 Soap-making ingredient
45 Twice-boiled Chinese snacks
47 Anthology series created by Ryan Murphy, for short

48 Genre for Korn and Slipknot
50 Drink pairing for salmon, perhaps
52 Charlotte Brontë's "Jane ___"
53 Vanishing Asian sea
54 Loo
56 Location of Caesars Palace
58 Mega
60 Playable sets of cards, in rummy
62 Lazy-sounding star?
63 To whom the song "Do You Want to Build a Snowman?" is sung
65 Early Ron Howard role
66 Glassdoor posting
67 Like
68 Like Gotham after Mr. Freeze's attack, in "Batman and Robin"
69 Johto-region "Pokémon" professor

Answer on page 118.

Babies on Board

BY WILL NEDIGER

ACROSS

1 ___ sheet (resource for a freelancer)
5 "My voice should tell you who I am"
10 British alphabet enders
14 It's a thing in Italy
15 Baseball player Ryan honored by a set of commemorative Beanie Babies
16 Word in red on a sign
17 Tingle-inducing video genre
18 Play footsie, maybe
19 Water bobber
20 Brokers' business?
23 500 sheets of paper
24 Hopping mad
25 Nourishing stews, firm handshakes, etc.?
30 It'll show you the world
31 "___, I Shrunk the Kids"
32 ___ Lanka
35 Glasgow guys
36 Homes for some owls
37 Pioneering linguist Chomsky
38 Brazilian greeting
39 Word that would be "badder," if it was regular
40 Valuable monkey Beanie Baby whose name is also a drum
41 "Belongings" or "stuff"?
43 Movie franchise that inspired the Donkey and Gingy the Gingerbread Man Beanie Babies
45 Lift to check the weight of

46 Company behind Beanie Babies, or a hint to this puzzle's theme
52 Tiny amounts
53 Like a loud crowd
54 "The Parent ___" (1998 film starring Lindsay Lohan and Lindsay Lohan)
55 Shows on TV
56 Regard with contempt
57 Vibe
58 Color of Manny the Manatee
59 Moves slowly
60 Let borrow

DOWN

1 Sing like Betty Carter
2 Spice Girl with a pout
3 "God Help the Outcasts" singer, in "The Hunchback of Notre Dame"
4 José of the Three Tenors
5 Renown, but of the bad kind
6 ___-free numbers
7 Letter opener's creation
8 ___ Beth's Bean Bag World magazine
9 Twists together
10 Animals like Ziggy and Zig-Zag
11 Exhibit exuberance
12 Part of LED
13 "No matter how hard I might try / This place is simply a pig ___" (lines from the poem included with Soybean the Pig)

21 Grub

22 Bacchanal

25 Bear Beanie Baby with angel wings

26 "... plus some other people": Abbr.

27 Choreographer Twyla

28 Derby the ___

29 Descriptor for some demons

32 "That's just completely false"

33 Pasta sauce brand

34 "That's my cue!"

36 Where jackets might be lined up

37 Like a snakebite you'll survive

39 Tiny warbler

40 "Nailed It!" host Nicole

41 Overly prim

42 Parts of roses

43 Flight segment?

44 Many-headed monster

47 Waves the Whale is one

48 Animals like Pouch, casually

49 Prep for a fruit salad, perhaps

50 Merit

51 Cross-shaped feature of an N64 controller

52 Heart-shaped feature of a Beanie Baby

Answer on page 119.

Hot, Hot, Hot

BY KAREN LURIE

ACROSS

1 Greek letters
5 Vehicles for some zoo tours
10 Droid
13 Gevinson of 2021's "Gossip Girl"
14 Luck in La Laguna
15 Nail
16 Word before rock or rain
17 Tim Allen was the highest-paid one, in the '90s
18 Fox crib
19 (56-Across for my) cozy two-person sofas
21 "___, baby!" ("Swingers" catchphrase)
23 Shade of black
24 Undisturbed
25 (56-Across for) the author of "The Unbearable Lightness of Being"
30 Ferrell's cheerleading partner on "Saturday Night Live"
31 Salad dressing need
32 Hoax
36 Clear after taxes
37 (56-Across for my) platform where I do my little turn
41 Kimono sash
42 "Raspberry Swirl" singer Tori
44 Western Indian state
45 The feet a sonnet has (just like this clue)
47 (56-Across for your) like-minded political cohorts

51 Chi-chi caviar
54 Elliott on "The Bear"
55 Wood knot
56 1992 Right Said Fred hit
61 They're checked at the door
62 Talking-to
64 She said knock you out, per LL Cool J
65 Grind
66 Turkish capital
67 "Right the hell now!"
68 DJ's stack
69 En ___
70 Not so much

DOWN

1 Abbr. at the end of a list
2 Word before Tuesday or truck
3 Tel ___, Israel
4 Cognac cocktail
5 Fiji is the country closest to it
6 Take five
7 Crafts partner
8 NYC subway overseer
9 Waitperson
10 Merit award
11 View from Malibu Sands, on "Saved by the Bell"
12 Uptight
14 Outback order, often
20 Tails was his sidekick
22 Chapters of history
24 Peddle
25 Homer Simpson's mom

26 Couple in a gossip column
27 Jared of "My So-Called Life"
28 "In your dreams!"
29 ___ de los Muertos
33 iPhone button
34 Short form, for short
35 "___ Misery" (Elliott Smith song on the "Good Will Hunting" soundtrack)
38 Taj Mahal city
39 Tater ___
40 "King of the Web Brawlers" Slice
43 Egg (on)

46 Really, really bad
48 Sparkly
49 Grow more complex, as wine
50 Congo river
51 Breakdancer from a crew like the Lady Rockers
52 Turn out to be
53 Wears well
56 Grates on
57 Writers' degrees: Abbr.
58 Relaxation
59 Holiday six days before NYE
60 Puppy peeps
63 "Blonde" star ___ de Armas

Answer on page 119.

The X-Files

BY ERIN RHODE

ACROSS

1 Wedge
5 Org. that assigned "The X-Files: Fight the Future" a PG-13
9 One of the seven deadly sins
14 Prefix with cab or cure
15 Fish feature not pronounced like the first syllable of the name of the actress who portrays Scully
16 Singer Mann who played a nihilist in "The Big Lebowski"
17 Piece of punditry
18 "Scully, as you know, cats are normally carnivores, but this tailless one mysteriously survives on baked goods alone!"
20 Florida city
22 Peter, Paul, and Mary, e.g.
23 "Scully, someone ... an alien, I assume ... has wrapped this choir platform with a tight rubber cover!"
25 LOL alternative
29 Boom box
30 Clean Air Act, e.g.
32 Things to get over
36 Helpful
37 "Scully, this fancy watch is keeping time backward!"
41 It overtook Motorola as the best-selling mobile phone brand in 1998
42 Oar whose adjectival form, if it had one, would look like Mulder's partner
43 "Works for me"
45 Elite
50 Spring break?

51 "Scully, I don't know how this car keeps driving when its rear tires are connected by nothing but a pungent root!"
55 Like Coast Guard rescues
57 Piano perch
58 "Scully, something's happened to this portrait of President Washington! He's gotten ... squarish!"
62 Citation abbr.
63 Good, in Granada
64 Eye piece
65 Word after wild or dirty
66 Gluten-free alternative to beer
67 Taste ___ (the Pepsi challenge, e.g.)
68 Mufasa's brother

DOWN

1 Bobbins
2 Term for a cool guy that was dated even in the '90s
3 Think up
4 "Beaches" star Bette
5 Studio behind "Thelma & Louise"
6 First of 12 popes
7 Sporty Italian cars, for short
8 Title role for Michael and Jude
9 "I ___ to believe"
10 Joke cappers
11 Reddit Q&A, for short
12 "___ Things I Hate About You"
13 Base 16, for short
19 As to
21 Metal part of a chopping tool
24 Sauce thickener

26 Actress Shawkat
27 "The Kids in the ___"
28 What epic things inspire
31 They throw rocks at houses
33 "___ Doubtfire"
34 Chest muscle, for short
35 "Law & Order" spin-off that premiered in 1999
37 Type of IRA
38 Colo. neighbor
39 "Tha Block Is Hot" rapper
40 Otherwise
41 Something a critic might pick
44 Princess Fiona, eventually

46 Modern "toodles"
47 Non-native
48 Business end of a duck
49 Silent partner of a magic duo
52 "The truth ___ there"
53 Touchy spot
54 Items thrown down to challenge someone to a duel
56 Composer Stravinsky
58 Telly network
59 Nice way to say yes
60 Marked a ballot
61 "___ my shorts!" (Bart Simpson catchphrase)

Answer on page 120.

Lollapalooza Lineup

BY BRENDAN EMMETT QUIGLEY

ACROSS

1 With respect to
6 IT assistance, perhaps
12 Bulletin board material?
16 First line of attack
17 RNA component
18 Spinning rod on the road
19 Chunk missing from the sidewalk? (1995, 1995)
21 Valley with sloping sides
22 228 Peace Memorial Park capital
23 Actress Dennings
25 Sought a seat
26 Gross leftover after a meal of sole? (1996, 1993)
31 "A Series of Unfortunate Events" author Snicket
34 1991 John Grisham novel, with "The"
35 Presentation's support
36 Cult '90s band with the album "Spiderland"
37 Built like a jet
38 Carrying heat
39 Dave's rival in an Olympics-themed 1992 Reebok campaign (until he failed to qualify for the Olympics, whoops)
40 Class with makeup exams?: Abbr.
41 English channel, familiarly, with "the"
42 Wunderkind from a religious retreat? (1992, 1997)
48 Hook's mate
49 San ___ Capistrano
50 ___-A-Fella (record label co-founded by Jay-Z)
52 Safe spots
54 Standing out
55 Norwegian cruise sight
57 Persian person, presently
58 Torah holders
59 Seriously overcharges
60 Livestock farmers that don't play fair? (1997, 1994)
63 "Ice Age" protagonist
64 Spot for a plug
65 Northern region
68 Scott ___ (Seth Green's "Austin Powers" role)
70 24-hour span in a rainforest? (1992, 1994)
75 Get the cargo on the ship
76 Surname of screenwriting sisters Nora and Delia
77 Baudelaire verse?
78 Block of ice
79 Gets into hot water?
80 Makes an even exchange

DOWN

1 Many websites try to make you install one
2 Venetian blind piece
3 Bean enjoyed by Hannibal Lecter
4 Rarely used golf club
5 Widespread
6 ___ Wars (Carthage/Rome struggle)
7 Kind of TV that's far from a flatscreen
8 "It is to laugh! In fact, I just did!"
9 Prefix for system or sphere
10 Rapper discovered by the Notorious B.I.G.
11 Court responses
12 Schoolyard classic that comes in freeze and TV varieties
13 Heavy metal frontman known for wearing a kilt in the '90s
14 Sobered (up)
15 Where you might pick up a few pointers
20 One : four :: ___ : moe
24 Viking Eric's nickname
27 "Dear, ___ we're facing a problem ..." (lyric from the Cardigans' "Lovefool")
28 Bit of blue humor
29 Questlove's do, for short
30 Thumper's bud
31 It might make you see things

32 Placekicker Jason who scored a total of 17 points for the Broncos in their 1998 and 1999 Super Bowl wins

33 Daily New York Times puzzle

37 Start up a pot

38 "___ Flux" ("Liquid Television" segment)

40 Bumfuzzled

41 He was briefly engaged to Gwyneth in the '90s

43 Boy band whose debut single was "I Want You Back"

44 Verbal filler phrase

45 Throb

46 Pirate's booze

47 Days of ___ (time travel destination, perhaps)

51 Columbia House purchases in the '90s

52 Departure's opposite

53 Tied the knot

54 "Roll up the window!"

55 Grasping tool

56 "This second"

57 In and of ___

58 Like the series ending of "The Sopranos"

59 "Runaway Bride" star Richard

61 Locks that share their name with an Ivy

62 Fixes up holes

66 Noodle preparation?

67 ___ classic (movie like "Romy and Michele's High School Reunion" or "Spice World," e.g.)

69 World Wide Web creator Tim Berners-___

71 "___ Don't Use Jelly" (1993 Flaming Lips song)

72 Territory whose rulers included Charlemagne and Otto I: Abbr.

73 Dole's gp.

74 Fist-pumping cry

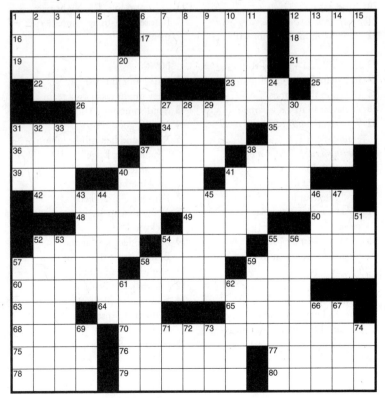

Answer on page 120.

Shuffling Decks

BY SID SIVAKUMAR

ACROSS

1 Member of a South Asian diaspora
5 Incense residue
8 Stringed instruments larger than violas
13 FBI ___ (many a role on "The X-Files")
15 Data-managing tech exec
16 Polynesian language with a 14-letter alphabet (plus 3 extra letters for loanwords)
17 *Complete VHS collection, maybe*
19 Conundrum
20 Steadfast
21 *Short-term financing arrangement*
22 Prefix with like, but not with love
23 Leonardo da Vinci's "Mona ___"
24 Indianapolis-to-Cincinnati dir.
25 Down in the dumps
28 Draw for Garry Kasparov
32 *Territorial conflict between rival groups*
34 *Pulling a rabbit out of a hat, e.g.*
38 Together, in music
39 Sound heard in a cave
41 Real estate unit
42 *What generous people have, so to speak*
45 *"I'll have another," in Spanish*
48 Doctor's instrument for the tongue
50 CPR expert
51 Glimpsed
54 Dustin Diamond didn't become one until the second season of "Saved by the Bell"
55 "The Magic School ___"

57 With 64-Across, collectible-based product lines such as Pokémon or Digimon ... or what the answers to three pairs of italicized clues are doing in this puzzle?
59 Pea jacket?
63 All up in flames
64 See 57-Across
66 Shed some feathers
67 What a snowboarder catches
68 "Fear of Flying" author Jong
69 Hog the vanity, say
70 Counterpart of "thx"
71 ___-motion ("The Nightmare Before Christmas" animation technique)

DOWN

1 Small amount to apply
2 They might clash on a team
3 Send something risqué, maybe
4 Not on good terms
5 Rock band behind the album "The Razors Edge" [sic]
6 ___ of relief
7 Tool used to till
8 Baroque choral piece
9 Name that spells a citrus fruit backward
10 Nickelodeon's splat and Blockbuster's ticket, for two
11 Some Tibetan monks
12 Laughably ridiculous
14 Fact that's plainly obvious
16 Playground installation with a fulcrum
18 App with Stories and Reels, familiarly

21 Video game character who can befriend a toilet (or, more commonly, other virtual humans)
23 Tres ___ cake
25 Shot in the dark
26 Luxury automaker that released the "A" series in the '90s
27 Pharma product
29 Number that only increases over time
30 Fuzzy growth on a tree
31 Swaths of history
33 "Family ___" (game show)
35 Highest point
36 Finally prepare for a final
37 Try out
40 Western Hemisphere defense gp.
43 GeoCities or AOL.com user

44 Uncorked
46 Dressed like a judge
47 Walk through deep mud, say
49 On the ___ (often, informally)
51 Something you buy to stick in a corner
52 Ann ___, Michigan
53 Pixar robot who has no elbows
56 Practices boxing
58 Bit of info that, if saved in the wrong format, could cause a Y2K bug
59 Go wherever the wind blows?
60 Makes a goof
61 Fail to mention
62 Art ___ (architectural style)
64 Beanie or snapback, e.g.
65 It's tapped from a tree

Answer on page 121.

Keep 'Em Separated

BY PAOLO PASCO

ACROSS

1 Walkman insert
5 Pestered persistently
13 Big name in historical impalers
17 Bart's teacher for 20+ years
18 "... at least, that's what it feels like to me"
19 Capital city hidden in "Brigadoon"
20 Certain fire signs
21 "Honestly ..."
22 "Let every creature go for broke and sing / Let's hear it in the ___ and on the wing" ("I Just Can't Wait to be King" lyric)
23 "That was soo funny ... not!"
25 Insects in the "My Girl" scene that traumatized a generation
26 Poseidon's realm
28 "You're not *that* great at hiding"
30 They bring Time money
31 The lower of two major landforms making up New Zealand
36 Fox Squishmallow with a repetitive name
39 Without wobbling
40 Train leading to the ring?
44 ___ Us (game with crewmates and impostors)
46 African country whose flag depicts a machete
47 A ledge, a statue, or conceivably any surface, for a pigeon
48 In all of recorded time
51 "Guts" contestant who successfully climbs the Aggro Crag, e.g.
52 Bank (on)
53 GPS "S"
54 "One fight ___ time" (fifth rule of Fight Club)
55 Word before a connecting airport, on an itinerary
57 [not my mistake]
58 Dir. that's 9-Down minus one letter

59 Hit '90s song whose title explains why there are three blank squares in this puzzle?
66 Strictness
68 Spot for a Manhattan-minded traveler?
69 "High-five me, baby!"
72 Golfer Lorena
73 2001 film whose protagonist works at the Café des 2 Moulins
74 Name in this puzzle's byline
75 "Baby Got Back" subject
76 Two-word tenet taught in an intro improv class, probably
77 "Whose Line Is It Anyway?" host before Aisha

DOWN

1 Territory home to India's capital
2 What a mind map helps organize
3 Go "Honk shoo, honk shoo"
4 Milks for bread?
5 Laughing gas, informally
6 Mo. in 1990 when the Hubble Space Telescope was launched
7 Vittles
8 "Well, I'll be!"
9 Direction 90 degrees clockwise from norte
10 "Isn't that obvious?" sounds
11 "What do you mean funny, funny how? How ___ funny?": "GoodFellas"
12 What an all-nighter might lead into
13 Pieces of technology in "The Lawnmower Man" or "eXistenZ"
14 The "you" in "You are sixteen, going on seventeen"
15 Say "Yes, the Spice Girls are also my favorite band of all time," maybe
16 Papas
24 Edebiri of "The Bear"
27 QVC competitor

29 State where "Touched by an Angel" was set
30 God with 99 names
32 Justin Timberlake or JC Chasez, vocally
33 Home of the International Court of Justice, with "the"
34 Teen ___ (Jonathan Taylor Thomas or Sarah Michelle Gellar, in the '90s)
35 Like a fertile river delta
36 Decree issued in the "Rushdie affair"
37 Dramatic cry from a war movie extra
38 In vain
41 One who's there for demonstration purposes?
42 "A Thousand ___" (1997 movie based on a Jane Smiley novel)
43 "You know you got the mad phat fluid when you ___" (lyric from "Halftime" by Nas)
45 Revolutionary who shares his first name with the narrator in "Evita"

47 Get pumped
49 Expression from someone doing the "DreamWorks face"
50 "That true?"
56 Unable to attack
57 Show off, like Santana
60 (Old) codger
61 Not too racy
62 What huge lodes have huge loads of
63 West coast sch. where some "Buffy" episodes were filmed
64 "Am I my brother's keeper?" asker
65 Device at some café checkout counters, nowadays
66 ___ Thomas (artist featured on Santana's "Smooth")
67 Area in some "Chicago Hope" episodes, for short
70 Grand ___ Opry (venue that inducted Alison Krauss as a member in 1993)
71 Comic book fight scene onomatopoeia

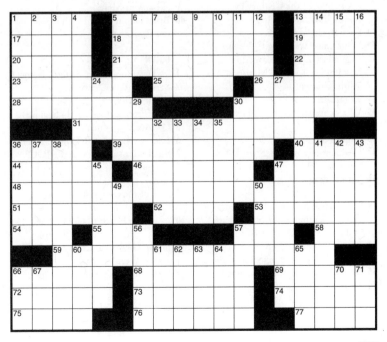

Answer on page 121.

U-Turns

BY FRANCIS HEANEY

ACROSS

1 "The ___" (1994 Denis Leary/ Judy Davis movie)
4 Easy-to-catch ball brand
9 Basics
13 Letters read by beachgoers?
16 Put one's ___ in (opine)
17 Halved
18 Soda that sounds like a sock
19 "Just found this out ..." acronym
20 Pitcher who threw a no-hitter for the Kansas City Royals in 1991
23 Palindromic brand in the kitchen
24 Lip balm brand
25 Beetle Bailey's superior
26 Elf on a cereal box
27 From ___ to dusk
29 Actor who debuted as Spike on "Buffy the Vampire Slayer" in 1997
33 Muhammad who was named Sportsman of the Century by Sports Illustrated in 1999
34 New Rochelle college
35 What those watching Q-V see?
36 Legendary DJ who played himself in a 1995 episode of "Married ... With Children"
41 Complain about
45 Wax extremely enthusiastic, colloquially
46 Unpleasant aroma
47 Williams who won her first U.S. Open in 1999
48 Titular dragon in a 1998 PlayStation game
49 "Untouchables" star who voiced Agent Flemming in 1996's "Beavis and Butt-head Do America"
51 Impressed interjections
54 You can't pass anything without them
55 McClanahan of "The Golden Palace"
56 Director with the 1997 autobiography "A Mad Mad Mad Mad World: A Life in Hollywood"

62 "Don't ___ on me" (inscription on a winter toy invented by Benjamin Franklin in a "Simpsons" dream sequence)
63 Target for Nick Faldo
64 Deliberately ignores
65 Judge Lance who became suddenly famous in 1995
66 Half of deux
67 "I Want It That Way" band (and how you might describe 20-, 29-, 36-, 49-, and 56-Across)
73 Some of the thoroughfares in this puzzle can be found there: Abbr.
74 Cambodian currency
75 Weapons in silos
76 Part of RSVP
77 "You should be ashamed"
78 "Let me just ___ word of advice ..."
79 Planet first seen in 1999's "Phantom Menace"
80 Brian who recorded with U2 as the Passengers

DOWN

1 "A Few Good Men" director Reiner
2 Serving of corn, perhaps
3 Black-and-white movie of 1993?
4 "___ From a Rose" (1994 Seal hit)
5 "We were ___ break!"
6 Place to wager on 8-Downs: Abbr.
7 Stockholm's country, to the IOC
8 Target of whispering in a 1998 movie
9 50% of the cost of something expensive?
10 "___ on a Beach of Gold" (1995 Mike + the Mechanics album)
11 Show whose characters periodically appeared on "Wings"
12 It might be original, mortal, or deadly
13 Sharon of "Basic Instinct" and "Casino"

14 "Toy Story" studio
15 Movies like 1993's "Super Mario Bros."
21 32,000-ounce weight
22 "Andre the Giant ___ a posse"
26 "SNL" self-help guru Smalley
27 Basically everybody, to Randy Jackson
28 Thrown for ___ (dazed)
29 Bossa nova legend Gilberto
30 ___ Taylor Loft (store that debuted in 1998)
31 Rank of George Clooney's character in "Three Kings"
32 Underline or italicize, say
34 "Don't worry about me, man"
37 E.g.
38 "Much ___ About Nothing"
39 Core of a 2-Down
40 ___ Krunch (short-lived cereal of the 1960s with freeze-dried dessert bits)
42 "DuckTales" inventor Gyro
43 How actors say lines
44 "___ Lunch" (1991 Peter Weller/Judy Davis movie)

47 Internet suffix for Nap or Friend
50 Bread that may have seeds
52 One side of a certain argument
53 Having audio and video matched up
56 Push aside
57 "Rent" won four in 1996
58 Smart ___
59 "___, Fran, and Ollie" (early children's TV show)
60 Some offensive linemen: Abbr.
61 "Rudy" star Sean
62 Letters on a choral work with no alto line
65 "Is ___ hard to believe?"
67 Madonna sported a pointy one in 1990
68 Company that's the namesake of a set of red, white, and yellow plugs
69 Flow back from the shore
70 Comedian Philips who appeared on "Dr. Katz, Professional Therapist"
71 Yang's counterpart
72 ___-Blo (fuse brand that touts its longevity)

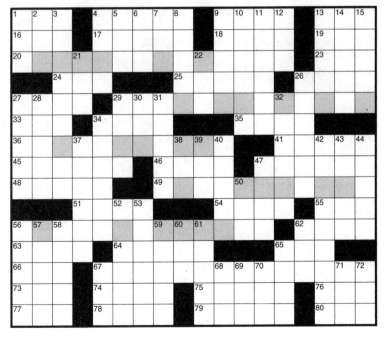

Answer on page 122.

Crunch Time

BY ALEX EATON-SALNERS

ACROSS

1 Perched upon
5 Nirvana's "Come as ___ Are"
8 Sissy of "JFK" and "Affliction"
14 Hippodrome racers
16 A gourmet's is refined
17 Capturing the moment, briefly
18 Toward the back, on a boat
19 Hippodrome outfits
20 Old NYC subway line commemorated by a Subway sandwich
21 Start of many California city names
22 Helen who played Queen Charlotte in "The Madness of King George"
24 Having achieved a photogenic state
26 Comply with commands
27 Fluff, as bangs
29 U2 hit single of 1992
30 Tell an untruth
31 Answer to "You saw that too?"
33 Ford flop
35 1995 action comedy "___ Boys"
36 One with a revolting personality?
40 Tuna type
43 Food label fig.
44 It was sometimes less than a dollar per gallon in the '90s
46 Beyond silly
47 Hangs heavy
48 Ones ensuring a clean sweep?
50 Vampire killers

52 Help ticket holders find their seats, slangily
53 Quayle and Gore, e.g.: Abbr.
54 "Blue's Clues" host Burns
55 Video editing software for Macs released in 1999
57 1996 movie starring Michael Jordan ... or a hint for three squares in this puzzle
60 PBS game show villain Sandiego
61 What Bill Clinton totally didn't inhale
62 Works, as dough
63 Consumed
64 Abba who narrated the 1992 TV documentary "Israel: A Nation Is Born"

DOWN

1 Word after class or circus
2 "___ Crossroads" (Bone Thugs-N-Harmony hit of 1996)
3 Acorn droppers
4 Type of monastary
5 Stretchy exercise clothes
6 Big name in elevators
7 Rose Bowl winner of 1990 and 1996
8 Sent unwanted emails to
9 Counterpart of cut or copy
10 ___-rock (genre for the Pixies or Radiohead)
11 Type of birth
12 Online investing option
13 "Oh my God! They killed ___!"

15 Pulitzer Prize-winning "Picnic" playwright
20 Derived from
22 Chomper of plant roots
23 "Ditto," in footnotes: Abbr.
24 Venezuela's capital
25 Enjoyed a merry-go-round, say
28 Kevin who succeeded Branford Marsalis as leader of the Tonight Show Band in 1995
31 Feeling flush and feverish, say
32 Pique
34 Right on point?
37 Meineke service
38 Competitive advantage
39 "I am a ___ who alas loves a lad ..." ("Sweeney Todd" lyric)
41 Some writing implements
42 Say again
44 Counterpart to a maid of honor
45 Fresh off the cruise ship
47 "He-e-e-elp!"
48 Roadmaster maker
49 Like Harvard's halls
51 Private eyes, in old slang
54 Fitting name for a Dalmatian
56 MTV prize that the Smashing Pumpkins won six of for "Tonight, Tonight" in 1996
57 Place for a pedicure
58 Initials before an alter ego
59 1992's "A Few Good ___"

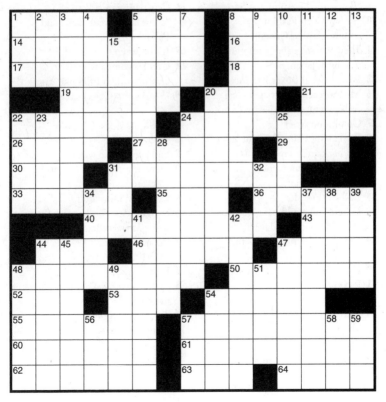

Answer on page 122.

Floppy Discs

BY QUIARA VASQUEZ

ACROSS

1 Digging up dirt on political rivals, familiarly
5 The start of something
10 Snoozes
14 Court mate of Jordan?
15 Palmer who promised, "I'll see you in 25 years" (and she did—thanks, Showtime!)
16 Home state for the Breeders and for Brainiac
17 Items collected when starting a puzzle, often
19 Dark ___ (retro art style seen in "Batman: The Animated Series")
20 "In My Own Fashion" autobiographer Cassini
21 They operate a soy sauce museum in Chiba, Japan
23 Former Mail Boxes Etc. location
26 Missouri sch. that's the oldest college west of the Mississippi
27 Common carrier
28 Prefix with chute (but not ladder)
30 Go back, in a way
32 Prefix for phenomenon
33 Janitor's appliance
34 Billboard fodder
38 Where you could hang out with "Friends" on Thursday?
39 "The Iron Giant" voice actor Marienthal
40 Use one's freedom of choice
41 Pro
42 "Coneheads" star
44 Nat ___
45 Thing cut down and covered in tinsel, often
46 She might say "What a sty!"
47 Nice way to feel
49 Often-mispronounced sandwich
50 Member of one target audience for this book
52 Remaining
54 Phrase like "rosy-fingered dawn" or "wine-dark sea" (or, in another sense, "stupider like a fox")
58 Easy equine pace
59 Test taken (and aced) by Carol Hathaway on "ER"
60 Genre for A.L.T. and Cypress Hill
64 Dope
65 Make a rebound, say
66 City with namesake 1993 "accords" between Israel and Palestine
67 It's between first and third
68 Comics company with creator-owned titles like "Spawn"
69 "Freaks and Geeks" creator Paul

DOWN

1 ←
2 Sight for whale watchers
3 Devices rarely used by a spring chicken?
4 Common ultimatum
5 System with two or more (but not many more) sellers
6 When repeated, a "Martin"-inspired dance craze
7 Easy mark
8 "... ___ saw Elba" (end of a famous palindrome)
9 To-do list fodder
10 Ska-punk band whose keyboardist Eric Stefani quit to work as an animator on "The Simpsons"
11 [Shut up and listen to me]

12 News unit?

13 "How ___ Is Now?" (Smiths song a.k.a. the theme from "Charmed")

18 Animal companion

22 Perennial pilferer

23 "Revolutionary Girl ___" (notable 1997 anime cited as a major "Steven Universe" inspiration)

24 Quickly visit

25 Word that follows "Big" and "Grand" on Michigan maps

29 High point

31 TV franchise in which almost every episode involves the raising of stakes?

33 An 18-Down who wants fresh milk, perhaps

35 It's too hot to handle

36 Bête ___

37 Problem caused by bugs

43 "Sleeping in My Car" duo

48 City in upstate New York where Tommy Hilfiger was born

49 Vanish

51 Wednesday Addams portrayer

53 Buttload

54 "_arru___!"

55 Eight, in Ecuador

56 Title of authority

57 Total phony

61 Watch part

62 "Fresh Prince of Bel-Air" actress Tatyana

63 Fruit juice brand (and namesake of a kids' game of the '90s that involved trying to get stacked discs to flip)

Extended Finales

by Karen Lurie

ACROSS

1 Put up with
6 Profound, man
10 Something of concern to Groundskeeper Willie
14 Ho Chi Minh Museum city
15 Sicilian spewer
16 Lady Gaga's was pink with green filling
17 Sphere
18 Slog
19 African river
20 Tend to, as an overgrown 10-Across
21 "Oh man, I overdid it with the audacity there"?
24 Arizona native
25 Place for a "No Soup for You!" iron-on decal
26 Giving lessons to budding Louis Armstrongs?
32 Lent a hand
33 It can be barefaced
34 Defrost
37 Stack of Post-its, e.g.
38 Withdrew
42 French monarch
43 Cozy
45 Matt Foley lived in one down by the river
46 Pub order
48 Keeps the lights on at a certain spelling competition?
52 A fake one looks orange
53 Boss of fashion
54 '90s R&B group that wanted to sex you up, and whose spelling rubbed off on 21-, 26-, and 48-Across

59 Tool played with a bow
62 Obsessed captain
63 Easy-Bake ___
64 Last letter of Lemnos?
66 Surfer's stop
67 Big name in rolling?
68 "Designing ___"
69 Did some weeding, say
70 Wapitis
71 "Bring in 'da ___, Bring in 'da Funk"

DOWN

1 Total con job
2 Poi base
3 From the top
4 ___ sequitur
5 White ___ (fragrance introduced by Elizabeth Taylor in 1991)
6 Hold back
7 English prep school
8 Oklahoma city
9 Where to find a date
10 Most time-consuming
11 Met melody
12 "___ make it better the second time around" (end of the "Step by Step" theme song)
13 "Great British Bake Off" co-host Fielding
22 Pen prefix for emergencies
23 Word often heard before "verily"
24 Hustle, quaintly
26 Activates, as a phone icon
27 "Glass Onion" director Johnson
28 Be logical
29 Secluded valleys
30 Auction action

31 Something Edward Scissorhands might turn into topiary
35 Top-notch
36 Sweeping
39 Extra extra?
40 Word before pool or wash
41 Force into a bad sitch
44 Turn in for the night
47 Prefix for an ENT
49 Card game whose rules can be explained in less than 1% of the time it takes to explain Magic: The Gathering

50 Sarcastic "gee" follower
51 Cabinet dept.
54 Benjamins
55 Birthplace of seven presidents
56 Behind
57 Like a soap opera twin, often
58 He proclaimed himself a loser in 1994
59 Vehicle driven by Large Marge in "Pee-wee's Big Adventure"
60 Matures
61 Diminish
65 Cow commentary

Answer on page 123.

Harvesting Crops

BY CHANDI DEITMER

ACROSS

1 Keep risotto from sticking, say
5 Play to the back of the house
10 Hot sauce ingredient, as it's often spelled in product names
15 Natural resource source
16 Deliver a speech such as "Women's Rights Are Human Rights"
17 Made of gold
18 "Should ___ acquaintance be forgot ..."
19 ___ B. Latimer, founder of Federally Employed Women
20 Maiden, Mother, and ___ (Triple Goddess of neopaganism)
21 Nancy Drew and the Hardy Boys, in an amateur sense
23 "Killer ___" (song by the Beets with the line "I refused to touch that strange bean curd")
24 Cards from college?
25 Ink storage spot
28 Smoking vessel
30 Good connections
31 Item in many a springtime basket
34 Scarfed down some Shark Bites, say
35 "Diamond Lil" playwright West
36 Pro who budgets and balances, for short
37 Fix
38 "Loser, loser, double loser, whatever, as if, get the picture, ___!" (schoolyard chant)
39 Cropped '90s fashion trend ... depicted literally throughout this grid
41 Return addressee?: Abbr.
42 Green start
43 Fashion house that Tom Ford began overseeing in 1999, for short
44 Real so-and-so
45 "Celebrity Jeopardy" show

46 Group whose '90s members included Britney Spears, Justin Timberlake, Christina Aguilera, and Ryan Gosling
49 "Eat Drink Man Woman" director ___ Lee
50 Contentious '90s rap figure Knight
51 One's digits, for short
52 "Glass House" singer DiFranco
53 Perlman of 1996's "Matilda"
55 1987 lower-body workout tape that sparked a trend lasting into the '90s
61 Set-up man, of a sort
62 Cuban capital
63 Good or good-looking
64 Follow
65 Keep things juicy, in a sense
66 Addition word
67 Features on some classic cars, such as the Pontiac Firebird and Trans Am
68 Classic Fender guitar, familiarly
69 Tamagotchi and Furby, e.g.

DOWN

1 ___ bracelet (accessory that might leave a mark)
2 U2's "Zoo TV," e.g.
3 Treat served with sambar
4 Treat akin to a Twizzler
5 Facial features of *NSYNC's Chris Kirkpatrick and the Backstreet Boys' AJ McLean
6 Charles de Gaulle alternative
7 Christian who played Laurie in 1994's "Little Women"
8 "I'm telling you!"
9 "Well, golly!"
10 Successful result of negotiation between nations
11 Icy moon of Jupiter

12 Illegal activity by the prison labor–exploiting warden in "The Shawshank Redemption"
13 Britney in a locker, maybe
14 Role for Jim before "The Mask"
22 Targets of many 45-Across parodies
26 All-___ pass
27 Deals (with)
29 Messy food items used in a prank on "Salute Your Shorts"
30 "My suspicions were right!"
31 Dial-up connectors
32 "___ Dude" (Nickelodeon series)
33 ___ Posadas (December observance)
34 In the know
35 Props in the "Are You Afraid of the Dark" episode "The Tale of the Many Faces"
38 Political gp. that included "Blue Dogs" in the '90s
39 "Toodle-oo!"

40 Pavement cover material
45 Dismiss loftily
47 Escorts, as to a loft
48 Magazine that traditionally had a slew of boys with mushroom cuts on the cover
49 Stretch from enero to diciembre
52 That's a good point
54 Agreements, in session
56 Country that saw less than 20% of the '90s: Abbr.
57 ___ bene ("Look here!" in legalese)
58 Isolate
59 Itty-bitty, like anything owned by Polly Pocket
60 They're drama queens, according to astrologers
61 Tamagotchi or Furby, virtually speaking
62 "Ghostwriter" airer

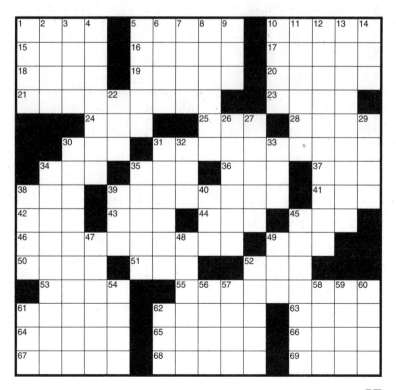

"Hello, 62-Across..."

BY PAOLO PASCO

ACROSS

1 Like the smell of a stink bomb
6 "Curb Your Enthusiasm" channel
9 Dog accessory that might be shaped like a bone
14 "___, Vincent. ___" (Elaine's tearful reaction to watching a good movie recommended by video store employee Vincent)
15 What a metal Pog Slammer resembles
16 Moving day rentals
17 Costanza, after becoming much less stocky?
19 Evince embarrassment, maybe
20 Like the name Bookman for a librarian
21 Events in Jerry's life, vis-à-vis Jerry's act?
23 "___ she blows!"
24 "The Tonight Show" host before Carson
25 Friend of Pooh whose name rhymes with "Pooh"
26 Direction opposite NNW
29 Acrobat's one-piece garment
34 Magazine read by Jackie Chiles?
37 "Welp, gave it my best"
38 Attack, as Jon Voight does to Kramer in "The Mom & Pop Store"
39 Big brutes, figuratively
41 Little brutes, figuratively
42 Chew out, and how
44 Limits on the allowed number of Festivus decorations?
46 Pierce of "Mrs. Doubtfire"
48 The apartment in "Seinfeld" or the apartment in "Friends," e.g. (I guess '90s sitcoms loved apartments)
49 Road turnaround, informally
50 Lena who played an assassin in "Romeo Is Bleeding"
52 "Auld Lang ___"
54 "Kramer, write down that you saw me take a chair"
59 System ___ Down
62 "Seinfeld" character known for popping up unwantedly
63 Pet name for Elaine?
65 Colored ring, in botany
66 "That trilobite didn't know an ___ from an elbow": Squidward Tentacles (in the "SpongeBob" episode "Band Geeks")
67 Piaf played by Marion Cotillard in a biopic
68 Like Fruit Gushers
69 Last the longest in "The Contest," e.g.
70 Lauder lauded by cosmetics fans

DOWN

1 "___ Gold: Greatest Hits" (1992 compilation album)
2 ___ circles (phenomena seen in "The X-Files")
3 Participate in the "airing of grievances," essentially
4 School like Harvard or 36-Down
5 Boxer's exhibition?
6 Prominent instrument in ska
7 Nickname for Dallas
8 Respond to "I ran a four-minute mile" with "Oh cool, I actually ran a three-minute mile," say
9 "There's that sound"
10 Frank Costanza and Morty Seinfeld, etc.
11 Backtalk, informally
12 Grogshop options

13 "Tug of Words" channel, for short
15 Make rougher
16 City college study?
18 "when are u getting here?" text
22 Multiple-time NBA All-Star Gasol
23 Folded stack in a hotel bathroom
25 4:3 or 16:9
27 No-___ album (record with all banger tracks)
28 "___ World" ("Sesame Street" segment with a crayon-drawn intro)
30 "Drag Race All Stars" champion Mattel
31 Mann with the 1995 abum "I'm With Stupid"
32 Individual leg lifts, e.g.
33 Deg. for someone who knows the drill?
34 "You're full of baloney!"
35 Treat yourself at a restaurant?
36 Harvard's opponent in "the Game"
38 Palindromic "one sec" letters

40 "What do we have here ..."
43 Blip
45 "The Andy Griffith Show" character who raised Opie
47 Zero
51 "Zero chance, buddy!"
53 "Whoopee!"
54 Michael who played George Michael Bluth
55 Wilson who played a serial killer in 1999's "The Minus Man"
56 Pollution with a portmanteau name
57 Mongolian desert
58 Part of, as a plot
59 "Consider the job done, boss!"
60 Fancy-schmancy party
61 Athlete to whom Jackie Robinson wrote, "Proud of your greatness as a tennis player, prouder of your greatness as a man"
62 Turner who led a revolution
64 Sassy's Jane Pratt et al.: Abbr.

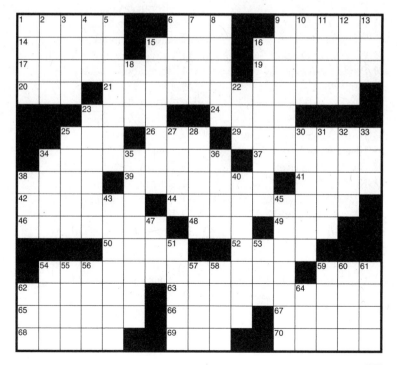

Answer on page 124.

Bridge & Tunnel Crowd

BY ROSS TRUDEAU

ACROSS

1 Band in "energy dome" hats
5 Frankenfood: Abbr.
8 With 16-Down, small '90s toys inspired by Scandinavian folklore ... several of which can be found hiding in this puzzle
13 Unsettling stare
15 Where expats live
17 Devils from day one
18 Cooks up a whopper for?
19 Brain tests, briefly
20 Doesn't guess, say
22 ___ Aviv
23 Ample
25 Passing votes?
26 Interactive tweet function
27 Stamina
28 German chancellor Scholz
30 Products such as the 1999 robot dog Aibo, e.g.
31 View from a deck, maybe
32 British singer Rita
33 British novelist Anthony
35 "I've already left!"
37 Blocked, as a river
41 Reef predators
42 "What is this, amateur night?!"
44 "Roger that, cap'n"
45 Andean crop
47 Ethical thought experiment involving a rail switch
51 Cry made with an upraised arm from a school desk
52 Univ. aides

53 ___ and void
54 ___ goal (undesirable soccer score)
55 Nasty cut
57 Skin layer
59 Highway speed limit enforcement warning
62 Dandy accessory, perhaps
63 Brainchild
64 Adult education gp.?
65 Boxers without managers?
66 "Ooh, sex-ay!"
67 Phishing target: Abbr.

DOWN

1 Interior Secretary Haaland of the Biden administration
2 Actress Mendes
3 Guitar Hero guitar, e.g.
4 "Full House" small pair?
5 Troops at ease?
6 Admin
7 1994 Olympic gold medal figure skater Baiul
8 Sings
9 Softball stat
10 If I mine it, it's mine
11 Over the head of
12 In recent memory
14 Brand for artist Nathan Sawaya
16 See 8-Across
21 Chewy dinner bread
23 "Oh, and ..."
24 Many a TikToker

26 Maya Angelou's "On the Pulse of Morning," e.g.
29 Install, as brick
30 "Treat yourself" site
32 Duolingo's Duo, for one
34 Pot emanation?
36 "Mm-hm"
38 They might say "You Are Here" to shoppers
39 Bag removers?
40 AOC, for one
42 Ever so narrowly
43 Photo ___ (Kodak moments)
45 Appropriates

46 "Hang on, better idea"
48 Site with a crafty marketing strategy?
49 Like some garages
50 Word incessantly rhymed with "sir" in "Hamilton"
55 "Greetings, fellow Aussie!"
56 Basics
57 He co-starred with Diedrich, Christa, Ryan, Kathy, and Craig in a '90s sitcom
58 Ultrafan
60 GPS prediction
61 Civil rights icon ___ B. Wells

Answer on page 125.

That Sinking Feeling

by Francis Heaney

ACROSS

1 Units with a "fan only" mode, for short
4 Slaughter's rank, on "G.I. Joe": Abbr.
7 "___ on ..." (recurring "In Living Color" sketch)
10 Gear projection
13 "The 'T' in ___ does not stand for 'terrorism'" ("Fox & Friends" correction, on "SNL") (it actually stands for "tomato")
14 "All Quiet on the Western Front" setting, briefly
15 Name that sounds like part of a roof
16 Los del ___ ("Macarena" duo)
17 Ignition inserts
19 Auto company that's an anagram of one of the words that YSL stands for
21 Lair ... [iceberg rips a hole in the hull] ... Get dimmer
22 "Must-see TV" time slot for "Seinfeld"
23 Spew lava
24 Wises up about
27 "The Replacement Killers" star Chow Yun-___
28 Duo
30 ___-ching (cashing-in sound) ... [passengers run for the life rafts] ... Actress Kiernan
31 MacArthur ___ ("Genius Grant" recipient)
33 Plenty
34 Purpose of many items bought at The Container Store
37 Paris Hilton, e.g.
40 Madonna's "___ Don't Preach"
41 Like eddies or soft-serve ice cream
43 Places to attend Smashing Pumpkins concerts
46 Word before hygiene or history
47 Something to plug a guitar into

50 Part of a certain religious garment
52 "___ Beacon Teaches Typing"
54 "___ Better Blues" ... [Jack doesn't try nearly hard enough to fit next to Rose on that door] ... ___ mule
55 Deception
56 Chain with ads that featured "spongmonkeys" singing "WE LOVE THE SUBS!!!"
58 1997 movie about a big boat that sank ... which is the same thing that's happened to three boats in this puzzle
59 "___! The Cat" (animated series of the '90s)
60 Blown up, like a photo: Abbr.
61 "___ was saying ..."
62 Sch. near the Maine state line
63 Manic Panic, e.g.
64 Old car company that produced the Speed Wagon
65 "The Ballad of Peter Pumpkinhead" band
66 "Hang On to Your ___" (Beach Boys song covered by Frank Black in 1993)

DOWN

1 Pre-G string
2 "Doctor Who" companion played by Jenna Coleman
3 Work it on the runway
4 Flower that a "Popeye" character was named for
5 Nickname for actress Paltrow
6 "Whether ___ nobler in the mind ...": Hamlet
7 Reason to receive a scholarship
8 Squares up
9 "Money Love" singer Cherry
10 Fall apart under pressure
11 Upton Sinclair novel that "There Will Be Blood" was based on
12 "You've ___ Mail"

18 GI's potato-peeling duty
20 Where the bees are
22 Roman emperor who succeeded Claudius
24 "Buffy" librarian and mentor of the "Scooby Gang"
25 "It's time to stop the fight" decisions
26 Feeling one's ___ (getting a little cocky)
29 Prerequisite for geom.
31 Muppet performer who directed 1999's "Bowfinger"
32 Tilt-a-___ (carnival ride)
34 Subject of many online haiku in the 1990s (one of mine was "In the thawing snow, / The can's blue corner peeps out / Like spring's first crocus")
35 What's the poi, really?

36 Performance with a sign-up sheet
38 "I'm entering my villain ___"
39 1994 Nas album
42 "Dang"
44 Ed who made a cameo appearance as Lou Grant on "Roseanne"
45 Biscuit that might be topped with clotted cream
47 Barbie Fashion ___ collection (1995 toy line debut)
48 Bogging down
49 Classic horror film remade by Gus Van Sant in 1998, for some reason
51 Scandinavian capital
53 Letters before an alias
55 Arthur's is seen in a popular meme
56 Latin initials in math class
57 Illegal highway maneuver, slangily
58 Receipt add-on

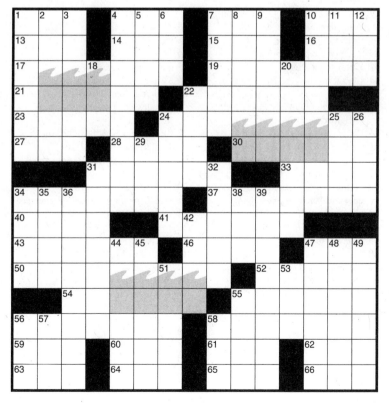

Answer on page 125.

Wooden Personality

BY TYLER HINMAN

ACROSS

1 "Incidentally," on ICQ
4 Character on "Da Ali G Show"
9 Visibly displeased person
16 Exclamation accompanying 28-Across
17 January 1, 1970, for Unix systems
18 Either of a T-shirt pair
19 Part 1 of a '90s Nickelodeon jingle
21 Recorder by a door or on a dash
22 Logic adverb
23 Part 2 of the jingle (and its singer)
25 Cubicle fixtures
27 Evince drunkenness
28 Exclamation accompanying 16-Across
29 "The House of ___" (1997 Parker Posey movie)
31 Helvetica alternative
34 Some '90s rappers, briefly
37 Part 3 of the jingle
43 CGY's in-province NHL rival
44 Buttload
45 Singer who spent her '90s as a child in Barbados
46 Part 4 of the jingle
51 Louis, Jerry, Bobby, Al, Johnny, Al Jr., Robby, or Al III of racing
52 Start of a Santana hit
53 "I think I've answered your question," on a message board
54 Cos. register them
55 Dispensers of wisdom
58 Interest limiter
60 Con's opponent
63 Russia last had one in 1917
64 Part 5 of the jingle
66 Reproductive cells
68 Something in a Sazerac
69 Guitarist Freeman who founded the Rippingtons
70 Part 6 of the jingle
74 Big name in racket sports equipment

76 Got down (from)
77 Wrote in a way that's very difficult to erase
78 She may add to your shopping list
79 Indian VIP
80 Capital whose country changed its name with the U.N. in 2022
81 Frequent cocktail finishers
82 Extraction operation, in brief
83 Kept the king from being poisoned, say

DOWN

1 Like the heads of people showing respect
2 Manager who won his first World Series in 1996
3 Henry Clay and Daniel Webster, for two
4 Honey Nut Cheerios' mascot is one
5 Pulls the trigger (for)
6 With "the," band that released "Do You Want More?!!!??!" in 1995
7 Soccer club that won five Scudetti in the '90s
8 They performed "Burn" for the soundtrack of 1994's "The Crow"
9 "___ Town" (Killers album named for a casino)
10 Second word in a rhyming nickname for a humanities course
11 Everything in old Rome
12 Word in a multiple-choice question
13 Do battle
14 Carrier at TLV
15 "Ratatouille" protagonist
20 74-Across's headquarters
24 Kardashian matriarch
26 They might be buzzing with excitement?
30 Sound that nasal strips might prevent
32 Hardly dense
33 CCCV ÷ V

35 ___ Pool (punnily named biology teacher in "Sabrina the Teenage Witch")
36 Scorch in a frying pan
37 Frequent bank freebie
38 Five-star review in poem form
39 "The Ultimate Driving Machine"
40 What you might use in this book if you're confident
41 Haunted house sounds
42 Franz's partner on "Saturday Night Live"
47 Menacing statement to an upcoming opponent
48 Quantity of tobacco (and pretty much nothing else)
49 Word often followed by itself with a B added
50 Existing only on paper
54 Be criticized

55 AIM message sent before signing off
56 Airer of "Duckman" and "Weird Science" in the '90s
57 Punk pioneers who sang "I Wanna Be Sedated"
58 Help go viral
59 Prefix in body preservation
60 Find hilarious
61 "Yay, my stuff arrived!"
62 Inscription on a mug bought in June
64 1999 role for Keanu
65 Feats of Harry Blackstone Sr. or Jr.
67 Walker's home state, in a '90s series
71 Harald's predecessor on the throne
72 Totenberg of NPR
73 Landmark in eastern Sicily
74 1967 American League MVP, to fans
75 Exclamation heard over tapas, maybe

Answer on page 126.

Catch 'Em if You Can

BY QUIARA VASQUEZ

ACROSS

1 Nontoxic type of acid
6 Mineral used in drywall
10 He plays Edward's alter ego (spoilers!) in "Fight Club"
14 Meal
16 Like teams resolving a tie, for short
17 "Wayne's World" actress Skye
18 Roman emperor of the 9th century
20 "Don't take that ___ with me, young man!"
21 "___ Espinado" (duet with Maná on Santana's "Supernatural")
22 "Aladdin" character with a turban
23 Fruits first cultivated over 11,000 years ago
26 Sidewalk surfer
28 Righteous Babe Records founder DiFranco
29 Ooze (through)
30 ___ room (area with a pool table and a Playstation, maybe)
31 Magic: The Gathering action indicated by rotating a card 90 degrees
34 Afghanistan's capital
36 Common undergrad degs.
38 Colorado city named after a form of light entertainment?
40 "Living Single" actress Alexander
41 Symbol on Radioactive Man's uniform, on "The Simpsons"
43 Actress Deschanel whose film debut was in 1999's "Mumford"
44 Button next to START on a Game Boy
46 "Aladdin" character with a fez

47 Texas rock trio whose lineup stayed the same for 50 years
48 "She's So High" singer Bachman
49 Korean automaker
51 "My Family" actor Morales
53 Chicken ___ king
54 See 65-Down
56 Type with a slant, for short
57 Comic book character who goes by the superhero name Sub-Mariner
60 Divine namesake of yoga's Monkey Pose
62 ___ to a crawl
63 Video game where players photograph colorful critters— six of which are loose in this grid!
67 Prefix with cast or shadows
68 Iowa city that's not Iowa City
69 Call it a night
70 "I Got 5 on It" drug
71 Camera part
72 Dance that's as easy as 1-2-3?

DOWN

1 Shape of "the moral universe," per MLK
2 "I could care less"
3 Beer with a punny name like "Hoppy Gilmore," often
4 People asking "Hey, where can a fella get some drugs 'round here?"
5 Capital city where Ibsen lived
6 The Gits' frontwoman (1965–93)
7 Heavy, valuable brick
8 "Roseanne" family surname
9 Had some Fruit by the Foot, e.g.
10 Attacked with teeth
11 It's behind the front teeth

12 '90s tennis prodigy Kournikova
13 Like a ___ in the headlights
15 Hardly loquacious
19 Singer and anti-apartheid activist Miriam
22 Here come the warm jets
23 Most unbelievable
24 Russia is #1 ... this way, anyway
25 It helped many WWII vets go to college
27 Stephen of "The Crying Game"
29 One who's hardly a careerist
31 Greet with a car horn
32 Fancy term for a nipple ring?
33 eBay subsidiary until 2015
35 Instrument for Israel Kamakawiwo'ole
37 Quality of an AA meeting?
39 "Frasier" producer

42 Heist site in "The Thomas Crown Affair"
45 "___ the Fifteenth Season" ("Simpsons" Christmas episode)
50 Not out, in a way
52 Knight wear?
54 Got around via blades?
55 Like a sturdy tree
56 App with filters, familiarly
57 "Don't open this while the boss is around" letters
58 ___ vera
59 "Keep it coming!"
61 Fresh way to start
63 Arthur Read's "friendly" dog
64 Bupkis
65 With 54-Across, professional repairing a ripped canvas, perhaps
66 Candy that comes from the neck

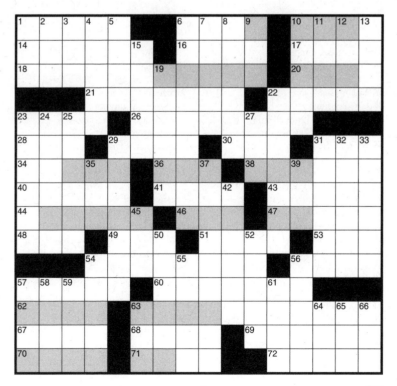

Answer on page 126.

Blast From the Passed

BY CHANDI DEITMER

ACROSS

1 Archaeological tourist site located in Wadi Musa
6 Rabbits' feet
10 Flight regulatory org.
13 Cable TV award, once
16 Vibes
17 "Faster! We're losing this drag race!!"
18 Space neighbor
19 L.A. Looks hair product
20 Slunk surreptitiously
21 College sports channel
22 Fight (for)
23 Blonde beverage
24 Heyerdahl craft
26 Event with clowns and ropes
28 Ape or parrot
30 'Til
31 Open the door to
33 Convenience of some onesies
35 Cider base, sometimes
36 Greek letter that looks like a O with a sideways I in it
37 Hasbro bro?
38 Creamy soup
40 ___ the farm (goes all in)
41 Thompson of "Howards End"
45 Mop of the morning?
48 One showing the ropes
50 Feeling of deep ick
51 Mythological Labyrinth savior
52 Scouse is a dialect of it: Abbr.
53 The end of the universe?
55 Property bothers?
56 ___ de mayo
58 Like many restaurant twosomes
59 For fear that
60 Left at sea?
61 Ruined
63 Savanna herd member
65 Makes whoopee, à la Austin Powers
66 Ring
70 Thatcher and Blair, for two
73 Alternative nickname for Nat, often

74 Magazine whose title is a pronoun
75 "My bad!"
76 ::blush::
78 Ocean-dweller with a 54-Down
80 "What's My ___ Again?" (1999 Blink-182 hit)
81 Torah storage spot
83 ___ horribilis (how Queen Elizabeth II described 1992)
85 Floods an inbox, say
86 Prompt
87 Bambi's mother, for one
88 Not hold back from
89 Skirt sort
90 "___ All That" (terrible 2021 remake of a 1999 rom-com)
91 She/___
92 Gaelic
93 Sap

DOWN

1 Call it a day
2 It contains about 23% of Russia
3 Size up from a venti
4 Dangerous dinosaurs ... or is it parentless male turkeys who pay close attention?
5 Piedmont sparkler
6 Faux ___
7 FBI operative ... or maybe it's a polite chap who performs serpent ceremonies?
8 Ryder of "Edward Scissorhands"
9 Heartthrob
10 Man likely to snag the presidential candidacy ... or, wait, perhaps it's everyone's preferred karaoke MC?
11 1990 Boxing Hall of Fame inductee Muhammad
12 Up to speed?
13 Best effort
14 Salsa star Cruz
15 Put into office, as Clinton in 1992 and 1996

17 One helping negotiate an insurance plan, perhaps ... or is it a dealer in Erté prints for Japanese hostesses?
25 Chris of "A Night at the Roxbury"
27 Double-___ sword
29 Iconic line of a 1999 Shyamalan film ... or the puzzle author's explanation of the confusion about 4-, 7-, 10-, 17-, and 40-Down
32 Beer cask
34 Mimosa mixers, casually
39 Massive dictionaries, for short
40 Prejudiced jerks ... or is it my parents' sisters, who wear black lipstick and enjoy partners across the gender spectrum?
42 Like an untouched Beanie Baby
43 Silencing phone button
44 Town home to Herky the Hawk
45 Prop on the set of "Air Bud"
46 The "E" of HOMES
47 Goes the way of Malcolm Crowe in "The Sixth Sense" (hopefully spoilers are okay at this point)

49 Chapel Hill sch.
50 "Shoppe" descriptor
54 Cephalopod trait, usually
57 Gaelic
60 Jason Biggs was caught in a compromising position with one in a 1999 movie
62 Discman power sources
64 Saudi capital
65 Craig or Smokey in "Friday," for two
67 Madrid-based periodical whose name in English is "The Country"
68 "Saved by the Bell" characters, eventually, e.g.
69 Abate
70 Prep, as an egg for a Benedict
71 Rule-breaker
72 Some bout weapons
77 Ivy with Elis
79 Bygone Bulgarian ruler
82 Sushi topper
84 Country that turned 20 in 1991: Abbr.

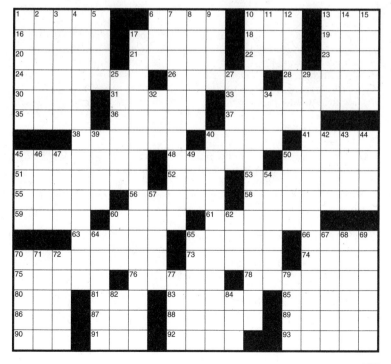

Answer on page 127.

#2 Hit

BY PAOLO PASCO

ACROSS

1 Head covering that may be worn with an eye veil
6 Firefox company
13 Vine watcher's site? (This would be trickier if the app Vine still existed)
18 1978 Nobelist Sadat
19 Like outdoor dining
20 Piece of headwear for Sailor Moon
21 One cracked to make a breakfast burrito
22 Hazard, as a guess
23 Phrase jokingly added after fortune cookie fortunes
24 Generate, as a CGI image
26 The Gay Nineties, e.g.
27 Watch cartoons all day, say
28 Mr. ___ (Elaine's onetime boss, on "Seinfeld")
30 Terra ___ warrior
31 Beau ___ (noble action)
33 "___ to Britney Spears, Ending in a Flood" (Hanif Abdurraqib poem)
34 Smirnoff alternative
35 "Get outta here, ya pest!"
36 Not 58-Down, 58-Down: Abbr.
37 Class that students might Zoom through?
40 Chicken ___ masala
42 "Dog Day Afternoon" shout
44 Motion-sensing Nintendo controller
45 Tractor brand that sounds expensive?
47 "Let There Be ___ ... Ruff Ryders' First Lady" (1999 debut album)
48 Aimee whose song "Wise Up" was featured in "Magnolia"
49 Fill-in worker
51 "Uh, yuh-huh!"
53 Fail, in an onomatopoeic turn of phrase
55 "That meme's so me"
57 Seafood eaten with crackers?
59 Store that was the "staple of 1990s normcore fashion," according to an article by The Independent

60 Org. '90s kids will all be eligible to join in a couple decades (feel old yet?)
62 Hopper "down undah"
63 "I'll take that as ___"
64 Total jerkwads
66 Feeling evoked by an artsy French film, stereotypically
67 Street haunted by Freddy Krueger
68 1D : linear :: 2D : ___
71 Group whose first letter stands for "T-Boz"
72 Stab or shot
74 Horses' fathers
75 "Boy Meets World" character who marries Cory in the final season
77 The Olsen Twins, etc.
80 Costar of Michael (multiple times) in "Multiplicity"
81 Gets even on behalf of
82 Cap
83 Scientist with an eponymous coil
84 Word before overload or deprivation
85 Rita Repulsa, to the Power Rangers

DOWN

1 Likely response to "Hey, wanna help rewind all these Blockbuster tapes?"
2 Shiba ___ (Japanese dog breed)
3 Their middle rows read "ASDFGHJKL"
4 Subject of the book "Talking Back, Talking Black: Truths About America's Lingua Franca," for short
5 They're worth a few bucks at rodeos?
6 Get an emotional reaction from, to say the least
7 "What's ___, Arnold?" ("Hey Arnold!" episode in which the main characters see "Carmen")
8 Calmer than calm
9 Acura model cited as an example of "when they try and mangle a positive word into a car name," in a "Seinfeld" stand-up bit
10 Winner's wreath

11 Turkish coins
12 Second word of "I Want It That Way"
13 Beefing
14 "XS" singer/songwriter Sawayama
15 Debut single for Britney Spears ... and a hint to this puzzle's theme
16 Frozen food brand named after two states
17 Comedian Gilda who won a posthumous Grammy in 1990
25 Capital of Qatar
27 Appear to be
28 Winter clock setting at LAX
29 "Just yanking your chain"
32 Car Seat Headrest album whose cover depicts two figures hugging
36 "Yo VIP, let's kick it" rapper, casually
38 M3GAN, e.g., for short
39 Madonna and Dennis Rodman, once
41 God with an unrequited love for Xena
43 Green plant at Brown
44 2020 song with the lyric "Macaroni in a pot"
46 Jocular suffix for "most"
48 Prop for Will Hunting, in the beginning of "Good Will Hunting"

50 "Lunches, brunches, interviews by the ___": The Notorious B.I.G., "Juicy"
52 "Everybody's Free (To ___ Sunscreen)" (Baz Lurhmann spoken-word hit)
53 Containers lugged by some stranded drivers
54 Like the statement "Salt-N-Pepa was a trio"
56 Sub's counterpart
57 Washes gently against
58 Surfing the information superhighway
59 Ballpoint alternative
61 Clearasil target
65 "Good Eats" sight
66 Champing at the bit
69 Cicierega whose song "Aaron" remixes "That's How I Beat Shaq"
70 Like Tom Hanks, for most of "Captain Phillips"
73 Aleve target
75 U. #2's
76 Gp. like Doctors Without Borders
78 What a show-offy slam-dunker hangs from
79 Place to go hog wild?

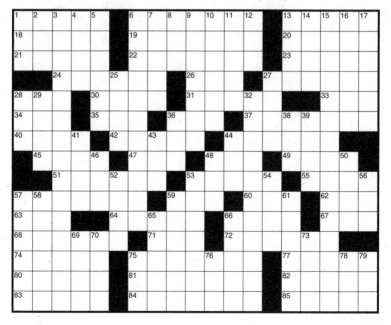

Answer on page 127.

Secret Agents

BY HOANG-KIM VU

ACROSS

1 It's something to shoot for
4 Pattern for Cher Horowitz
9 Restlessness
14 Certain file extension
15 Phrase on a Wonderland cookie
16 Froot ___
17 The 1994 Oslo Accords, for one
19 "Fast, Cheap & Out of Control" documentarian Morris
20 Permit
21 With 23-Across, orange hybrid
23 See 21-Across
24 Word before hall or up
27 66, e.g.: Abbr.
29 With 32-Across, Jenny McCarthy's replacement as host of MTV's "Singled Out"
32 See 29-Across
35 "8 Minute ___"
38 Overlook
40 Penne ___ vodka
41 Within the rules
43 Proficient
44 Prepare for a shot, say
46 "It's everywhere you want to be"
47 Starts from the ground up?
49 It replaced the Mini
50 "While you're ___ ..."
51 Attempt
52 With 55-Across, 1999 blockbuster, familiarly
55 See 52-Across
56 Whiskey variety
57 Like entrants in a certain derby
59 Home for the Mets for the 1999 playoffs
62 "Must See TV" network
65 Actress Hunt of "Mad About You"
69 Their intake is monitored in the South Beach Diet
71 Reserved for later
74 Jam out?
75 Here's a pointer!
76 Word in three Bond film titles (four if you count inflections)
77 With 78-Across, Will Smith blockbuster and song ... or a hint to three of this puzzle's squares
78 See 77-Across
79 The "S" in EST: Abbr.

DOWN

1 Half the name of an R&B trio
2 Jump for Kristi Yamaguchi
3 "The ___ World: Seattle"
4 Owner of a TV playhouse
5 Attendee at a stag do
6 Nibbled or noshed
7 Alternative to an 8-Down
8 Alternative to a 7-Down
9 With 28-Down, simple or uncomplicated
10 Opuesto del sur
11 That's a wrap!
12 Atop
13 Ireland or Britain, say
18 With 39-Down, responded to a Livejournal post, perhaps
22 Muck up
25 Thin strip of wood
26 Queen of Tejano music
28 See 9-Down
29 Take it easy
30 With 31-Down, "Glee" actress

31 See 30-Down

33 Steroid-free, as a baseball player

34 Targets with the Mutombo finger wag, say

35 Deep anxiety

36 Spartan

37 Politics and culture magazine founded in 1996

39 See 18-Down

42 With 58-Down, actress whose second movie was "A Night at the Roxbury"

45 One of Rabbit's pals

48 Michelle Yeoh's 1997 role Wai Lin, e.g.

53 Layer around a barn?

54 Haircut for Travis Barker or David Beckham

56 Hebrew for "master"

58 See 42-Down

59 '90s McDonald's Monopoly game, as it turns out

60 Hearty companion?

61 Activist Brockovich

63 Spill the tea

64 ___ Brashear (Navy diver whose life was depicted in "Men of Honor")

66 Mall staple named for a slang term for its primary merchandise

67 Revise a draft

68 "___ You Tonight" (INXS song)

70 1990 Nine Inch Nails single with the lyric "And your strain, it gets under my skin"

72 401(k) alternative: Abbr.

73 Certain file extension

'90s Freestyle

by Quiara Vasquez

ACROSS

1 Massive Attack album that raised the floor for hip-hop?
10 One of four in the "Friends" opening credits
14 Comedy film about the coolest guy in all of California?
15 "Don't Be a Menace to South Central While Drinking Your ___ in the Hood"
16 What Eagle-Eye Cherry isn't (!)
17 Part of a 20th-century armada
18 Judge Doom throws a shoe into one full of the Dip
19 Subject of the case "Galoob v. Nintendo"
21 "Romeo + Juliet" director Luhrmann
22 Elevations
23 Famous Amos?
24 "Hocus Pocus" director Kenny
25 Endings in "Super Punch-Out!!"
28 "The 11 O'Clock Show" character
29 Brown ones were popular in the '90s
30 Latin American steppe
32 Storage device first sold in 1999
34 Opened up more than just a crack?
35 Anne of the shot-for-shot "Psycho" remake
36 Nickname for 25-Down
39 ___ violation
40 "The Incredibly True Adventures of Two Girls in Love" star Nicole ___ Parker
41 "... and?"
43 "Get Smart" baddies
44 Least decrepit
45 Serpent with a pun-friendly name
46 It'll get you in hot water fast
49 Refrigerant blamed for the ozone hole: Abbr.
50 "To Live and Die in L.A." artist
51 Stuck in a Groundhog Day loop, e.g.
55 Mulder or Scully, e.g.
56 Bill Nye made one out of a soda bottle
57 "Satan Gave Me a Taco" singer-songwriter
58 "Cry me a river!" à la Livia Soprano

DOWN

1 "And every last inch of ___ covered with hair!" (musical boast by Gaston)
2 Otolaryngologist, but much, much shorter
3 Brand that loosed high-waisted pleated jeans upon the world
4 Something Scary Spice really, really, really wanted to have, or do, or ... something
5 Working without ___
6 It's declining in Paris
7 Shocking revelation from Mulan, maybe
8 Yogini's greeting
9 Buffy and Spike, sometimes
10 "Gelatinous" D&D creatures
11 Scar, e.g.
12 Smoothie berry
13 Either titular adventure-having character of a 1990s Nickelodeon series
15 Music fan who's "down with the clown"

20 Lang. of which Jules Vincent asked, "Do you speak it?"
21 More daring
22 Way to go?
23 Lieutenant ___ Yar of "Star Trek: The Next Generation"
25 Jennifer Jason Leigh flick about a town "the mob played ... like a smooth jazz riff"
26 "Cha Cha Slide" instruction
27 Surge, Slice, and Orbitz, e.g.
31 Handle, as rug rats
33 "Dis" ain't it
34 Big name in apples, or a street in the Big Apple
36 A big, dumb, balding North American ape with no chin (and a short temper)

37 Animal that your Fran Fine costume could also double as a costume for, probably
38 Rap impresario who founded No Limit Records
42 Bobby of the Bruins
44 Luxe
46 Machete mark
47 Titanic
48 Ecuador and Gabon left it in the '90s (but rejoined later) (and then Ecuador left again): Abbr.
49 Pattern for Lieutenant Dan
52 Deuteragonist of "The Tigger Movie"
53 He knows kung fu ... whoa
54 "Despicable Me" antihero

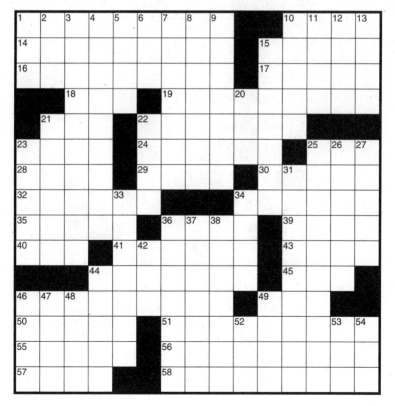

Answer on page 128.

Fashion Statement

P	U	T			F	I	L	M		S	A	L	T
E	G	O	S		U	B	E	R		O	W	I	E
C	H	O	K	E	R	N	E	C	K	L	A	C	E
		L	I	B			L	E	V	I	E	S	
S	L	A	P	B	R	A	C	E	L	E	T		
E	A	T		A	P	P	A						
A	R	E		S	C	R	U	N	C	H	I	E	S
M	E	N	T	E	E			T	O	N	A	L	
A	D	O	R	E			O	N	E	D	G	E	
P	O	W	E	R	B	E	A	D	S		O	L	E
		R	O	W	E			N	E	T	
	C	H	A	I	N	W	A	L	L	E	T	S	
I	G	U	A	N	A			L	O	S			
B	U	T	T	E	R	F	L	Y	C	L	I	P	S
E	R	I	E		D	E	A	R		L	A	R	A
T	U	N	S		S	E	W	S		N	O	D	

Seasoned Performers

X	E	N	A		H	U	L	A	S		P	S	A	S
J	E	D	I		A	N	I	M	E		O	T	T	O
S	C	A	R	Y	M	O	V	I	E		S	O	T	U
			B	U	S			S	C	H	L	E	P	
A	R	I	A	L		H	O	L		O	M	E	N	S
G	I	N	G	E	R	A	L	E		S	A	N	D	
E	L	K			E	R	E	A	D	E	R			
S	O	Y	B	E	A	N		P	I	C	K	A	X	E
		A	G	R	E	E	T	O			S	O	N	
	A	B	B	R		S	P	O	R	T	Y	S	U	V
O	N	R	Y	E		S	I	N		A	U	N	T	Y
P	A	I	D	T	O			T	N	G				
A	L	D	O		S	P	I	C	E	G	I	R	L	S
R	O	L	L		L	A	V	I	E		O	H	I	O
T	G	E	L		O	C	E	A	N		H	O	P	S

Step by Step

N	O	S	E			A	N	I	S	E		M	I	S
T	R	U	S	S		N	E	G	E	V		A	C	T
H	U	M	P	T	Y	D	A	N	C	E		I	E	R
		T	R	I	V	E	T		N	U	T	S	O	
E	T	O	I	L	E	S		A	T	T	A	I	N	
L	A	T	T	E	S		V	O	G	U	E	I	N	G
S	K	A			G	O	N	E	A	R				
	E	L	E	C	T	R	I	C	S	L	I	D	E	
		M	O	R	A	L	E			R	R	S		
M	A	C	A	R	E	N	A		M	E	D	U	S	A
A	R	R	I	V	E		M	A	D	E	M	E	N	
S	C	A	L	E		H	I	N	G	E	S			
C	A	V		T	O	O	T	S	E	E	R	O	L	L
O	D	E		T	R	A	M	S		D	E	L	A	Y
T	E	N		E	A	R	L	Y			S	O	B	E

Nick Names

A	P	E	S		S	P	E	C		F	I	S	T
S	O	L	E		E	A	R	P		A	S	T	I
S	I	D	C	A	E	S	A	R		T	A	R	E
		O	T	T	O	S		R	A	B	I	D	
C	U	R		E	U	G	E	N	E	L	E	V	Y
A	T	A	N		T	O	N	E	D		L	E	E
M	A	D	E			T	H	I	S				
P	H	O	E	B	E	B	R	I	D	G	E	R	S
		D	U	K	E			T	A	I	L		
A	P	P		G	E	E	N	A		S	R	T	A
G	E	R	A	L	D	F	O	R	D		P	E	P
E	L	O	T	E		T	R	I	S	H			
G	O	T	O		H	E	Y	A	R	N	O	L	D
A	S	I	N		P	R	E	Y		A	N	Y	A
P	I	P	E		S	E	T	S		P	E	E	L

First-Class Males

"You Go, Girl!"

Shuffle Play

Away Messages

Singing One's Praises

The Games of the '90s

Out at the Movies

Bill Collection

Screen Time

Tangled Yarn

Now That's What I Call Music!

D	U	O	S			P	S	S	T			T	L	C
A	S	A	P		M	E	T	O	O		O	R	E	O
D	E	F	I	N	I	T	E	L	Y	M	A	Y	B	E
				D	O	A		R	I	S	E	S		
N	E	V	E	R	M	I	N	D		N	I	T	R	O
I	C	E	R	A	I	N			O	I	S	E	A	U
R	U	N	S			A	I	S	H	A		H	R	T
V	A	T		F	A	N	M	A	I	L		R	E	M
A	D	U		I	N	E	P	T			L	A	G	O
N	O	R	W	A	Y			A	P	R	O	N	E	D
A	R	I	E	S		O	U	T	O	F	T	I	M	E
			I	C	A	H	N		W	I	I			
R	E	A	S	O	N	A	B	L	E	D	O	U	B	T
J	A	Y	Z		A	R	O	A	R		N	A	A	N
R	T	E			T	E	X	T			S	E	N	T

Pressing All the Right Buttons

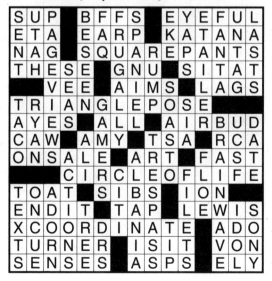

S	U	P		B	F	F	S		E	Y	E	F	U	L
E	T	A		E	A	R	P		K	A	T	A	N	A
N	A	G		S	Q	U	A	R	E	P	A	N	T	S
T	H	E	S	E		G	N	U		S	I	T	A	T
		V	E	E		A	I	M	S		L	A	G	S
T	R	I	A	N	G	L	E	P	O	S	E			
A	Y	E	S		A	L	L		A	I	R	B	U	D
C	A	W		A	M	Y		T	S	A		R	C	A
O	N	S	A	L	E		A	R	T		F	A	S	T
			C	I	R	C	L	E	O	F	L	I	F	E
T	O	A	T		S	I	B	S		I	O	N		
E	N	D	I	T		T	A	P		L	E	W	I	S
X	C	O	O	R	D	I	N	A	T	E		A	D	O
T	U	R	N	E	R		I	S	I	T		V	O	N
S	E	N	S	E	S		A	S	P	S		E	L	Y

Love Will Save the Day

T	H	E	N		S	S	T		A	B	B	O	T	S
V	A	L	E		E	E	O		I	R	O	B	O	T
S	T	R	O	N	G	E	R		M	O	R	I	T	A
E	C	O	N	O	M	I	E	S		W	I	S	E	R
T	H	Y		S	E	N		P	U	N	S			
		H	A	N	G	T	I	M	E		T	R	A
B	A	S	A	L	T		R	E	P		C	O	O	L
A	M	O	R	E		B	A	D		M	A	N	T	A
B	O	L	D		L	E	D		L	I	L	I	E	S
E	K	E		S	O	L	E	C	I	S	M			
		O	P	A	L		A	M	C		N	S	A
T	O	U	G	H		E	S	P	O	U	S	I	N	G
A	D	O	R	E	S		T	O	G	E	T	H	E	R
R	E	F	E	R	S		A	T	E		A	A	R	E
E	R	A	S	E	R		Y	E	S		C	O	D	E

Spikes Spikes Baby

S	L	I	P		A	T	T	I	C	S		S	F	O
P	E	P	A		D	E	E	P	L	Y		C	A	L
O	V	E	R	T	H	E	M	O	O	N		H	I	D
R	I	C	A	R	D	O			A	C	T	O	R	S
T	E	A	S	E		F	L	A	K	E	S	O	U	T
	S	C	A	N		F	O	R		D	E	N	S	E
		I	T	O		U	A	E		E	E	R	
	G	L	A	S	S	B	L	O	W	E	R		
M	I	R		U	T	E		N	O	M			
A	C	O	R	N		A	G	O		R	A	M	S
S	H	A	D	O	W	B	A	N		K	N	O	T	S
S	O	N	A	T	A			S	L	E	A	T	E	R
I	K	E		F	R	O	S	T	E	D	T	I	P	S
V	E	R		A	I	M	S	A	T		E	V	I	L
E	D	S		R	O	G	E	R	S		D	E	N	Y

Strike a Pose

O	D	E	U	M		A	V	I	V		S	A	Y	S
R	O	X	I	E		R	E	L	O		I	B	E	T
S	U	P	E	R	M	O	D	E	L		D	I	N	O
O	X	O		L	E	N	I		U	S	E	D	T	O
	N	A	O	M	I	C	A	M	P	B	E	L	L	
T	R	E	N	T	E		T	E	E					
P	E	N	N		S	C	A	R		D	E	B	I	T
K	A	T	E		Y	O	U		M	O	S	S
E	D	S	E	L		B	L	E	D		B	A	I	O
			T	I	E		A	L	E	R	T	S
C	I	N	D	Y	C	R	A	W	F	O	R	D
E	N	S	U	R	E		M	E	O	R		R	E	M
L	A	Y	S		B	E	T	T	E	R	W	O	R	K
L	I	N	T		A	A	H	S		I	D	O	N	T
O	R	C	S		G	R	E	Y		E	S	M	E	S

The One About...

D	A	T	A		S	P	E	A	R		N	O	S	E
A	B	E	L		T	E	R	R	E		I	D	E	A
M	A	R	S		R	A	M	I	S		N	E	X	T
	M	O	N	I	C	A	S	E	L	E	S		
		A	P	E		E	L	O						
D	E	R	I	V	E		L	E	A	D	E	R
O	V	A	R	Y		M	A	D		B	R	I	T	A
V	I	C	E		O	A	S	I	S		M	A	H	I
E	T	H		J	A	C	K	S	U	P		N	O	S
R	E	E	B	O	K		P	H	R	A	S	E
	L	I	E		P	E	G		O	U	R
T	I	Z	Z	Y		O	X	I		E	N	O	L	A
W	O	O	E	R		S	P	F		B	A	S	E	D
O	N	E	T	A	K	E		T	S	E	T	S	E	S
		M	E	I	O	S	I	S						
R	A	Y	M	O	N	D	C	H	A	N	D	L	E	R
B	R	A	I	N		O	H	O		O	U	T	T	A
G	E	O	D	E		N	O	P		W	O	R	D	Y

Solving the Night Away

Millennium Approaches

"1990s Game Shows for $200, Alex"

Move With Me

Clueless People

A	S	S	E	T		H	O	N	E			S	A	D	E
R	E	N	E	W		E	M	O	S		A	N	A	L	O	G
T	R	A	G	I	C	H	E	R	O		L	A	N	I	N	A
S	A	P		N	I	H	A	O		E	L	E	C	T	E	D
		E	N	E	R	O		M	E	E	T				
	B	F	F		C	H	A	M	B	E	R	M	U	S	I	C
B	A	R	R	I	O	S		O	R	G		S	I	K	H
A	D	A	I	R		A	N	G	I		R	N	A	
A	C	C	O	R	D	I	O	N	N	E	C	K	T	I	E	S
B	A	T		E	N	V	Y			C	R	A	W	S
A	L	A	S		S	H	E		M	E	L	A	N	I	E
A	L	L	E	G	I	A	N	T	A	I	R		P	O	T
		G	I	R	L		A	N	D	R	A			
T	V	M	O	V	I	E		M	S	D	O	S		A	M	P
H	E	A	V	E	N		J	E	W	E	L	T	O	N	E	S
E	R	R	I	N	G		O	R	E	N		I	N	D	R	A
M	A	Y	A			B	A	R	S		R	E	S	E	T

Finger-Lickin' Good

T	I	P	S			G	R	A	P	H		D	I	S
S	M	I	T	E		P	U	R	E	E		E	W	E
A	B	L	E	R		A	N	G	E	L		F	A	X
	R	E	P	R	O		D	O	L	P	H	I	N	S
E	O	S		O	N	S	E	T	S		O	A	T	H
S	K	I	P	R	O	P	E		O	P	E	N	T	O
P	E	N	D		A	P	L	U	S		T	O	P
		A	P	P	S		O	T	I	S			
U	F	C		C	A	M	P	S			A	C	A	I
P	R	O	M	P	T		H	E	L	I	P	O	R	T
F	A	N	S		O	S	I	R	I	S		O	M	S
R	I	N	G	P	O	P	S		D	U	P	L	O
O	D	E		U	T	A	H	N		C	L	A	I	M
N	S	C		T	I	M	E	S		K	E	I	R	A
T	O	T		T	E	S	S	A		D	R	E	W

The Crane-Beau Connection

G	A	S	S	Y			C	O	S	M	O		S	H	I	H
A	C	U	T	E		T	O	R	I	E	S		U	O	M	O
B	E	B	E	N	E	U	W	I	R	T	H		B	O	P	S
E	S	M	E		M	E	S	O		H	A	S	A	T	I	T
		A	R	A	B		L	T	R		A	R	I	S	E	
M	A	R		M	E	R	C	E	D	E	S	R	U	E	H	L
A	L	I		F	R	E	E		S	E	T	A				
D	E	N	I	M		A	R	T		A	H	C	H	O	O	
A	V	E	O		F	R	A	S	I	E	R		S	O	U	P
M	E	S	C	A	L		A	N	Y		D	I	R	G	E	
			N	E	S	S		C	E	D	E		N	H	L	
J	A	N	E	K	A	C	Z	M	A	R	E	K		R	T	S
U	S	U	A	L		A	A	A		M	E	D	I			
M	I	D	T	E	R	M		R	O	L	O		E	M	M	A
P	A	G	E		A	M	Y	B	R	E	N	N	E	M	A	N
I	G	E	R		J	E	T	L	A	G		A	T	E	I	T
N	O	S	Y		A	R	D	E	N		M	S	D	O	S	

Everyone's a Critic

S	I	G	N	S		N	B	A		B	A	J	A
O	M	A	H	A		A	I	L		A	G	E	S
B	I	L	L	Y	I	D	O	L		K	I	S	S
S	N	L		S	C	I		T	E	N	S	E	
		J	O	U	R	N	E	Y		G	E	T	
R	A	P	A			A	I	R					
A	M	A	N	A		G	I	N	A		M	O	E
J	O	H	N	M	E	L	L	E	N	C	A	M	P
A	R	K		O	X	E	S		T	H	R	E	E
			E	P	A			A	C	N	E		
P	O	M		B	O	N	J	O	V	I			
A	R	O	M	A		C	H	I		F	E	W	
I	N	X	S		A	E	R	O	S	M	I	T	H
N	O	I	R		B	Y	E		I	R	A	T	E
S	T	E	P		S	E	W		T	I	T	A	N

Get Psyched

O	C	T		H	O	P	S		L	I	O	N	E	L
P	A	H		U	M	N	O		U	M	P	I	R	E
E	M	U		M	A	G	N	U	M	P	I	N	O	T
R	E	N	N	E	R		I	S	E	E		A	S	S
A	L	D	E	R		S	C	E	N	T	S			
T	H	E	G	I	F	T		S	U	N	S			
E	A	R	L		R	U	S	S		S	E	I	S	
D	I	C	E		O	F	T	H	E		A	M	O	R
	R	A	C	K		F	L	A	P		K	O	L	A
	T	T	O	P			M	A	G	I	N	O	T	
	S	O	L	A	C	E		H	E	L	P	S		
A	S	H		K	I	L	O		W	E	R	E	I	N
S	P	E	C	I	A	L	K	N	O	T		B	A	E
T	U	R	E	E	N		E	G	O	T		O	N	S
I	N	S	E	R	T		S	O	S	O		N	O	T

You Oughta Know

T	U	P	A	C		L	A	S	E	D		F	O	M	O
E	V	E	N	S		I	L	U	V	U		R	U	E	D
A	L	A	N	I	S	M	O	R	I	S	S	E	T	T	E
S	A	C	S		H	E	H		E	T	H	E	L		
E	M	O		L	O	Y	A	L		E	D	I	T	S	
	P	A	Y	E	E		O	U	T	T	A		V	A	L
	T	A	N		N	E	G	E	V		H	E	I	R	
	M	A	Y	O			E	G	G	O					
B	L	T	S		S	T	A	N	D		O	L	D		
A	Y	E		E	L	I	H	U		A	L	E	R	T	
H	E	A	V	Y		S	M	U	R	F		Y	O	M	
	E	E	R	I	E		E	L	A		O	W	I	E	
J	A	G	G	E	D	L	I	T	T	L	E	P	I	L	L
O	L	G	A		O	S	C	A	R		L	I	N	E	D
B	A	S	S		L	A	Y	L	A		M	E	E	T	S

Babies on Board

S	P	E	C		I	T	S	M	E		Z	E	D	S
C	O	S	A		N	O	L	A	N		E	X	I	T
A	S	M	R		F	L	I	R	T		B	U	O	Y
T	H	E	R	E	A	L	T	Y	W	O	R	L	D	
		R	E	A	M			I	R	A	T	E		
H	E	A	R	T	Y	T	H	I	N	G	S			
A	T	L	A	S		H	O	N	E	Y		S	R	I
L	A	D	S		B	A	R	N	S		N	O	A	M
O	L	A		W	O	R	S	E		B	O	N	G	O
		P	R	O	P	E	R	T	Y	N	O	U	N	
	S	H	R	E	K			H	E	F	T			
	T	Y	I	N	C	O	R	P	O	R	A	T	E	D
T	A	D	S		A	R	O	A	R		T	R	A	P
A	I	R	S		S	C	O	R	N		A	U	R	A
G	R	A	Y		E	A	S	E	S		L	E	N	D

Hot, Hot, Hot

E	T	A	S			T	R	A	M	S		B	O	T
T	A	V	I		S	U	E	R	T	E		A	C	E
A	C	I	D		T	V	S	T	A	R		D	E	N
L	O	V	E	S	E	A	T	S		V	E	G	A	S
		C	O	A	L			S	E	R	E	N	E	
M	I	L	A	N	K	U	N	D	E	R	A			
O	T	E	R	I		O	I	L		S	H	A	M	
N	E	T		C	A	T	W	A	L	K		O	B	I
A	M	O	S		G	O	A			I	A	M	B	S
		P	A	R	T	Y	M	E	M	B	E	R	S	
B	E	L	U	G	A			A	B	B	Y			
G	N	A	R	L		I	M	T	O	O	S	E	X	Y
I	D	S		E	A	R	F	U	L		M	A	M	A
R	U	T		A	N	K	A	R	A		A	S	A	P
L	P	S		M	A	S	S	E		L	E	S	S	

The X-Files

S	H	I	M		M	P	A	A		W	R	A	T	H
P	E	D	I		G	I	L	L		A	I	M	E	E
O	P	E	D		M	U	F	F	I	N	M	A	N	X
O	C	A	L	A		S	A	I	N	T	S			
L	A	T	E	X	R	I	S	E	R		H	A	H	A
S	T	E	R	E	O			E	C	O	L	A	W	
		H	U	M	P	S		U	T	I	L	E		
	R	O	L	E	X	R	E	V	E	R	S	A	L	
N	O	K	I	A		S	C	U	L	L				
I	T	L	L	D	O			S	E	L	E	C	T	
T	H	A	W		G	I	N	G	E	R	A	X	L	E
		A	I	R	S	E	A		S	T	O	O	L	
B	O	X	Y	G	E	O	R	G	E		E	T	A	L
B	U	E	N	O		U	V	E	A		R	I	C	E
C	I	D	E	R		T	E	S	T		S	C	A	R

Lollapalooza Lineup

A	S	F	O	R		P	C	H	E	L	P		T	A	C	K
P	L	A	N	A		U	R	A	C	I	L		A	X	L	E
P	A	V	E	M	E	N	T	H	O	L	E		G	L	E	N
	T	A	I	P	E	I			K	A	T		R	A	N	
		R	A	N	C	I	D	F	I	S	H	B	O	N	E	
L	E	M	O	N	Y		F	I	R	M		E	A	S	E	L
S	L	I	N	T		A	E	R	O		A	R	M	E	D	
D	A	N		A	N	A	T		B	E	E	B				
	M	I	N	I	S	T	R	Y	P	R	O	D	I	G	Y	
		S	M	E	E		J	U	A	N			R	O	C	
	A	S	Y	L	A		B	O	L	D		F	J	O	R	D
I	R	A	N	I		A	R	K	S		G	O	U	G	E	S
T	R	I	C	K	Y	B	R	E	E	D	E	R	S			
S	I	D		E	A	R			A	R	C	T	I	C		
E	V	I	L		L	U	S	H	G	R	E	E	N	D	A	Y
L	A	D	E		E	P	H	R	O	N		P	O	E	M	E
F	L	O	E		S	T	E	E	P	S		S	W	A	P	S

Shuffling Decks

Keep 'Em Separated

U-Turns

R	E	F		K	O	O	S	H			A	B	C	S			S	P	F
O	A	R		I	N	T	W	O			N	E	H	I			T	I	L
B	R	E	T	S	A	B	E	R	H	A	G	E	N			O	X	O	
		E	O	S				S	A	R	G	E			S	N	A	P	
D	A	W	N		J	A	M	E	S	M	A	R	S	T	E	R	S		
A	L	I		I	O	N	A				R	S	T	U					
W	O	L	F	M	A	N	J	A	C	K			R	A	G	O	N		
G	O	L	O	C	O		O	D	O	R		S	E	R	E	N	A		
S	P	Y	R	O			R	O	B	E	R	T	S	T	A	C	K		
			O	O	H	S				A	Y	E	S		R	U	E		
S	T	A	N	L	E	Y	K	R	A	M	E	R		S	L	E	D		
H	O	L	E		S	N	U	B	S			I	T	O					
U	N	E		B	A	C	K	S	T	R	E	E	T	B	O	Y	S		
N	Y	C		R	I	E	L		I	C	B	M	S		S	I	L		
T	S	K		A	D	D	A		N	A	B	O	O		E	N	O		

Crunch Time

A	T	O	P		Y	O	U		S	P	A	C	E	K
C	H	A	R	I	O	T	S		P	A	L	A	T	E
T	A	K	I	N	GAP	I	C		A	S	T	E	R	N
	T	O	G	A	S		B	M	T		S	A	N	
M	I	R	R	E	N		C	A	M	E	R	AREA	D	Y
O	B	E	Y		T	E	A	S	E		O	N	E	
L	I	E		I	S	U	R	E	D	I	D			
E	D	S	E	L		B	A	D		R	E	B	E	L
		A	L	B	A	C	O	R	E		R	D	A	
	G	A	S		I	N	A	N	E		S	A	G	S
B	ROOM	S	T	I	C	K	S		S	T	A	K	E	S
U	S	H		V	P	S		S	T	E	V	E		
I	M	O	V	I	E		S	P	A	C	E	J	A	M
C	A	R	M	E	N		P	O	T	S	M	O	K	E
K	N	E	A	D	S		A	T	E		E	B	A	N

Floppy Discs

O	P	P	O		O	N	S	E	T		N	A	P	S
N	O	O	R		L	A	U	R	A		O	H	I	O
E	D	G	E	P	I	E	C	E	S		D	E	C	O
	O	L	E	G		K	I	K	K	O	M	A	N	
U	P	S	S	T	O	R	E		S	L	U			
T	O	T	E		P	A	R	A		E	B	B		
E	P	I		M	O	P		P	O	P	T	U	N	E
N	B	C		E	L	I		O	P	T		F	O	R
A	Y	K	R	O	Y	D		G	E	O		F	I	R
	S	O	W		S	E	E	N		G	Y	R	O	
		X	E	R		L	E	F	T	O	V	E	R	
H	O	M	E	R	I	S	M		L	O	P	E		
M	C	A	T		C	H	I	C	A	N	O	R	A	P
P	H	A	T		C	A	R	O	M		O	S	L	O
H	O	M	E		I	M	A	G	E		F	E	I	G

Extended Finales

S	T	A	N	D		D	E	E	P		L	A	W	N
H	A	N	O	I		E	T	N	A		O	R	E	O
A	R	E	N	A		T	O	I	L		N	I	L	E
M	O	W		M	E	A	N	D	M	Y	G	A	L	L
		H	O	P	I			T	E	E				
T	R	A	I	N	I	N	G	B	R	A	S	S		
A	I	D	E	D		L	I	E		T	H	A	W	
P	A	D		S	E	C	E	D	E	D		R	O	I
S	N	U	G		V	A	N		R	O	U	N	D	
		P	O	W	E	R	S	T	H	A	T	B	E	E
		T	A	N		H	U	G	O					
C	O	L	O	R	M	E	B	A	D	D		S	A	W
A	H	A	B		O	V	E	N		O	M	E	G	A
S	I	T	E		R	I	C	K		W	O	M	E	N
H	O	E	D		E	L	K	S		N	O	I	S	E

Harvesting Crops

"Hello, 62-Across..."

Bridge & Tunnel Crowd

D	E	V	O		G	M	O		T	R	O	L	L	
E	V	I	L	L	O	O	K		A	B	R	O	A	D
B	A	D	S	E	E	D	S		L	I	E	S	T	O
	E	E	G	S		A	S	K	S		T	E	L	
A	T	O	N	O	F		N	O	S		P	O	L	L
L	E	G	S		O	L	A	F		S	O	N	Y	S
S	E	A		O	R	A	TRO/LL	O	P	E				
O	N	M	Y	W	A	Y			D	A	M	M	E	D
	E	E	L	S		B	O	O			A	Y	E	
C	O	C	A	TRO/LL	E	Y	P	R	O	B	L	E	M	
O	H	O	H		T	A	S		N	U	L	L		
O	W	N		G	A	S	H		D	E	R	M	I	S
P	A	TRO/LL	E	D	B	Y	A	I	R	C	R	A	F	T
T	I	E	T	A	C		I	D	E	A		P	T	A
S	T	R	A	Y	S		R	A	W	R		S	S	N

That Sinking Feeling

A	C	S		S	G	T		M	E	N		C	O	G
B	L	T		W	W	I		E	V	E		R	I	O
C	░░	░░		E	Y	S		R	E	N	A	U	L	T
D	A	R	K	E	N		N	I	N	E	P	M		
E	R	U	P	T		G	E	T	░░	░░	░░		T	O
F	A	T		P	A	I	R		S	H	I	P	K	A
		F	E	L	L	O	W		A	L	O	T		
S	T	O	R	A	G	E		H	E	I	R	E	S	S
P	A	P	A			S	W	I	R	L	Y			
A	R	E	N	A	S		O	R	A	L		A	M	P
M	O	N	K	░░	░░	░░	L		M	A	V	I	S	
	M	O	S	C	O	W		F	A	K	E	R	Y	
Q	U	I	Z	N	O	S		T	I	T	A	N	I	C
E	E	K		E	N	L		A	S	I		U	N	H
D	Y	E		R	E	O		X	T	C		E	G	O

Wooden Personality

B	T	W		B	O	R	A	T		S	C	O	W	L	E	R
O	O	H		E	P	O	C	H		A	R	M	H	O	L	E
W	R	I	T	E	T	O	M	E		M	I	N	I	C	A	M
E	R	G	O		S	T	I	C	K	S	T	I	C	K	L	Y
D	E	S	K	S		S	L	U	R		A	H	H			
		Y	E	S		A	R	I	A	L		O	G	S		
P	O	B	O	X	N	I	N	E	S	I	X	T	H	R	E	E
E	D	M		T	O	N			R	I	H	A	N	N	A	
N	E	W	Y	O	R	K	C	I	T	Y		U	N	S	E	R
		O	Y	E		H	T	H		T	M	S				
G	U	R	U	S		R	A	T	E	C	A	P		L	I	B
T	S	A	R		N	E	W	Y	O	R	K	S	T	A	T	E
G	A	M	E	T	E	S		R	Y	E		R	U	S	S	
		O	N	E	O	H	O	N	E	O	H	E	I	G	H	T
Y	O	N	E	X		A	L	I	T		E	T	C	H	E	D
A	L	E	X	A		R	A	N	I		A	N	K	A	R	A
Z	E	S	T	S		E	V	A	C		T	A	S	T	E	D

Catch 'Em if You Can

A	M	I	N	O		M	I	C	A		B	R	A	D
R	E	P	A	S	T		I	N	O	T		I	O	N	E
C	H	A	R	L	E	M	A	G	N	E		T	O	N	E
			C	O	R	A	Z	O	N		J	A	F	A	R
F	I	G	S		S	K	A	T	E	R	A	T			
A	N	I		S	E	E	P		R	E	C		T	A	P
K	A	B	U	L		B	A	S		A	U	R	O	R	A
E	R	I	K	A		A	T	O	M		Z	O	O	E	Y
S	E	L	E	C	T		A	B	U		Z	Z	T	O	P
T	A	L		K	I	A		E	S	A	I		A	L	A
			R	E	S	T	O	R	E	R		I	T	A	L
N	A	M	O	R		H	A	N	U	M	A	N			
S	L	O	W		P	O	K	E	M	O	N	S	N	A	P
F	O	R	E		A	M	E	S		R	E	T	I	R	E
W	E	E	D		L	E	N	S		W	A	L	T	Z

Blast From the Passed

#2 Hit

Secret Agents

'90s Freestyle